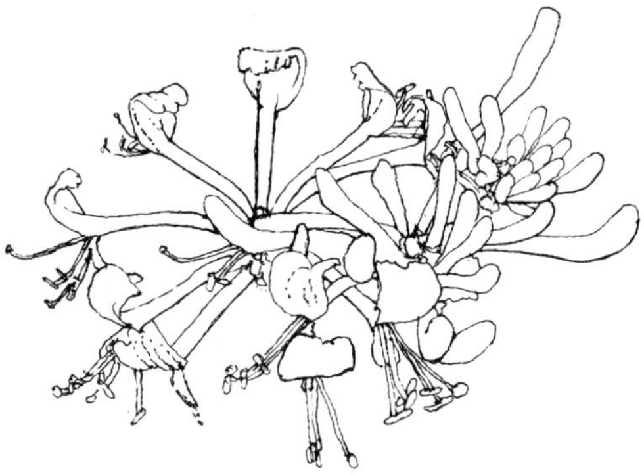

# POISONOUS PLANTS IN BRITAIN

## A CELEBRATION

**CHRIS HOWKINS**

Published by
Chris Howkins

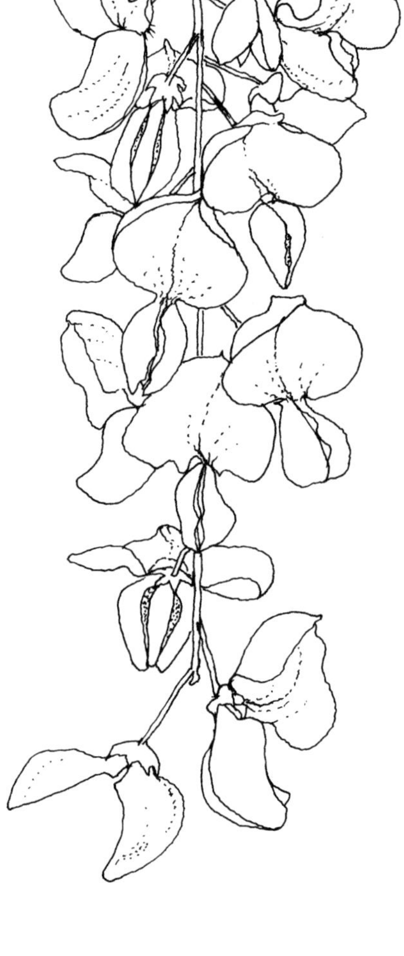



**PAPERBACK**
ISBN-10 1 901087 60 3
ISBN-13 978 1 901087 60 4
**HARDBACK**
ISBN-10 1 901087 61 1
ISBN-13 978 1 901087 61 1

**PUBLISHED**
Chris Howkins, 70 Grange Road, New Haw,
Addlestone, Surrey, KT15 3RH

**PRINTED**
Hobbs the Printers Ltd., Brunel Road,
Southampton, Hampshire, S040 3WX



**COVER PHOTOGRAPHS**
front – Delphinium, top-left – Ragwort, top-right – St John's Wort, centre – Border Iris

**CONTENTS**

## INTRODUCTION

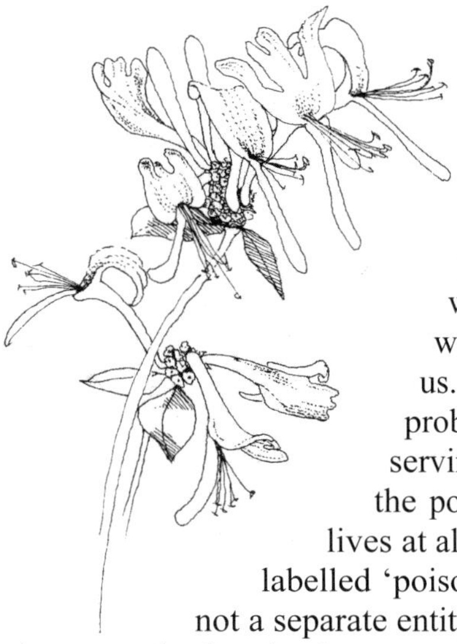

Dead Man's Fingers and Dead Man's Bells - oh what a gruesome picture a couple of plant names can paint! Lurking in the larder and waiting on the windowsill, growing in the garden and all along the walk with the dog is a menacing succession of plants that can poison us. Happily, we live quite safely with them and rarely run into problems. Indeed, we often enjoy them, from beautiful foxgloves to a serving of chips. Potatoes would not have any taste at all if it were not for the poison in them. If we stop to think about the plants in our everyday lives at all, then we are likely to have a separate little pigeon-hole in our brains labelled 'poisonous plants'. Such thinking does not really reflect reality. They are not a separate entity at all but are dispersed through our everyday lives, whether in rural, urban or suburban landscapes. There are dozens of different ones all mingled among the sights we may notice more clearly, among the birds and beasts, bridges and bungalows, bulldozers, buses and bikes. That has been reflected in the wide selection of illustrations for this book. There have always been people who knew which were the poisonous ones and how to exploit them, whether for ritual or for practical purposes. Back in the Bronze Age the shamans used Henbane to induce hallucinations for better communing with the gods. Until very recently every district seems to have had somebody, often a woman, who was skilled at herbalism. She was called upon to bring new villagers into the world, to treat their maladies through life and to lay them out at the end. What a wealth of knowledge has come down through the ages and upon this knowledge modern medicine has been founded. Dr William Withering had his curiosity aroused by the way a Shropshire woman used Foxgloves to treat oedema and his studies led directly towards today's heart medicines that use four of the poisons found in Foxgloves. With heart disease being currently one of the commonest causes of death in Britain just think how many people benefit from Withering's curiosity. By his time, in the 18th century, medicine was becoming more and more 'scientific' and was soon to expand dramatically with profound developments in all the sciences during the 19th century and beyond. It is from this period that most of the material presented in this book has been drawn. Only a few of us have much knowledge of what goes on in hospitals. We just expect one to be there when we need it and that its practitioners will do their job as effectively and as painlessly as possible. Some readers will be astonished to know that in the 'pre-med' before a general anaesthetic a patient is dosed with atropine from Deadly Nightshade. It is one of the deadliest poisons in any British wild flower. In skilled hands, however, it saves lives.

No doubt there was good reasoning for building this great flight of steps to a Wealden farmhouse but it does seem to isolate the people inside from the people in the lane outside – people who worked the land and knew how to satisfy their daily needs from it; people who had a sense of wonder for the natural world. Science today has tended to explain away people's sense of wonder, so there is something rather satisfying in discovering there are still plants in our everyday lives that are so complex that scientists do not fully understand them. Some questions are quite baffling. Why do some herbs work wonderfully in Chinese medicine and yet have the reverse effects when used in the West? So this is not a book about death and despair but a celebration; not a book about laboratories but about the plants in our lives and to that end many of the illustrations are contextual, giving little reminders of the landscapes and their features.

Plants produce poisons to safeguard themselves from being eaten or to save their seeds from being digested. Chemical warfare is just one of their strategies towards producing and dispersing their seeds successfully. These toxins have direct effects upon animals and man and these we have been learning to exploit for thousands of years – herbs to speed the heart, herbs to slow the heart, herbs to calm the brain and control epilepsy. The list is as long as the list of maladies from which we suffer. Most of the plants in this book have a long history in folk medicine but on the whole this has not been detailed. It would entail endless boring lists of maladies for which the plant's effectiveness as a treatment has not been verified. The emphasis has been upon treatments proven to be effective under modern clinical trials. Even so, not *every* application for each plant is given and omitted deliberately is the detailed information that might be sought for abortion, suicide, murder or terrorism. So repetitive lists of symptoms, maladies and uses have been avoided, especially as that information is now available readily on the Internet. Instead, this book is intended as a companion for those readers who enjoy exploring the wonders of the world around them and wish to extend their general knowledge and interest, so it is more of a celebration than a lamentation.

The intention was to produce a book that was interesting to browse through, whether looking at the sketches or stopping to read. Therefore, the usual format of an encyclopaedia has not been followed. The contents have been divided up into broad habitat categories, although in reality many plants pop up all over the place. They are all indexed. For most of the plant profiles the information has been organised around three key questions:- what are its poisons, what do they do and how are they used to our advantage? Even that format has been varied - we could not trace a use for Ragwort. Medical terms have been rendered in everyday English wherever possible, so *anthelmintic* would be expressed as *kills worms*. Obviously there was no avoiding the scientific names of the toxins, nor would it be desirable to do so, since they are valuable 'key words' for anyone wanting to reach the scientific websites on the Internet. There are a few words of guidance about that on the 'Sources' page at the end. Readers can easily skip the few technical lines if they wish. Staying on the subject of language, the English name of the plant has been rendered with an unfashionable capital letter, for the sake of clarity, which can be especially useful when the name begins with an adjective. Thus Green Hellebore is a specific plant rather than the greenery of any Hellebore while green Potatoes can be any Potatoes that are turning green.

The main emphasis is on the poisoning of humans. The toxins concerned affect mammals in general which should be borne in mind by readers interested specifically in pets and farm livestock. There are lots of references to these in the book but not always detailing the differing consequences between the different types of animal. The aim has been rather to heighten awareness and to go some way towards placing the plant in an agricultural context. So much of the traditional farming knowledge and lore is being lost as sons rarely take over the family farm these days. Many would say that the whole of British farming is dying. New farmers are being taught from a syllabus rather than the wisdom of granddad and so may not know which poisonous plants are prone to crop up in a particular corner of their land. People from entirely different backgrounds are escaping the stress of urban life for the countryside, to grow vegetables and keep a few hens or a sheep. These people too may not know the floral hazards around them. Raising awareness is important. Animals in our care need us to care.

Additionally there is a whole new nightmare of hazards arising with our children. For the last couple of decades feeding them has become increasingly a matter of supermarket produce and convenience foods, which has divorced the new generations from the natural product. Too many children cannot name the different fruits and vegetables when shown them. Few children are told not to eat the pips in their apple core. Coming to mind is a lady relating that her little grandchildren were playing 'safely' in the garden, except that one was feeding the other on 'sweeties' – the berries off an *Arum.* If we are going to teach children that fresh fruit and vegetables are good to eat then we must also teach them to be discerning. Those that are old enough to cook are also at risk since basic cooking lore is no longer passed on down the family line. Older readers will remember their mothers teaching them not to use green potatoes but it is quite alarming how few younger mothers today are aware of this danger. Lives are too busy for mothers to stop and teach their children to cook. Convenience foods have become so convenient! Now concerns are being raised over their healthiness if consumed excessively – too much sugar, too much salt, too much fat and so on. Consequently there is now a movement to encourage us all to return to using fresh fruit and vegetables far more often and to prepare our own meals. Gardeners have been preaching this already, for a couple of decades. Geoffrey Smith on the television caught people's imagine with his demonstrations of growing vegetables and salad crops among the decorative flowers while other presenters have shown how to grow food in window boxes and pots. This has been topped off more recently with an appetite for 'organic' produce. Thus it is important that we should know our plants. It is all very well knowing that Rhubarb leaves are poisonous but not much of a safeguard if children do not know what Rhubarb leaves look like. Supermarket Rhubarb is sold bereft of leaves.

Finally, but most importantly, sincere thanks are due to all the people over the years who have contributed to the database. Additionally, I should like to thank Dr Robert McGibbon and Stuart Salt for proof-reading the final draft and to Aaron Mason who worked hard checking the data and then converting text and illustrations into this book.

**What does poisonous mean?**

We all think we know what poisonous means but the more thought that goes into it the more uncertainty arises. The Oxford English Dictionary says a poison is, '*any substance which, when introduced or absorbed by an organism, destroys life or injures health.*' It adds that in popular usage it refers to '*a substance which destroys life by rapid action, and when taken in small quantity.* That, however, varies considerably, from person to person, and even between different examples of the same plant and even that can vary from year to year. We all know people who cannot eat strawberries, mushrooms, wheat or whatever, which introduces plants that cause allergic reactions. After some consideration, plants that cause allergies have been omitted, leaving those plants that have been long established as containing toxic compounds that affect everybody. Similarly omitted is the ever-increasing list of plants that are suspected of causing cancer. This book is not complete. Just because a plant is not included does not imply that it is safe. Primarily the book concentrates upon flowering plants, omitting all else, from ferns to fungi, but the Horsetails elbowed their way in because they occur in so many gardens and were once eaten.

**Woodworking**

This book does not include material concerning possible hazards arising through the handling of timbers or inhaling the dust during woodworking. A list of known timber hazards, naming trees and their health effects, is published by the Health and Safety Executive. Some entries highlight a possible danger from lichens of the bark which should be noted by woodworkers handling timber in its raw state. Woodworkers should be aware of the serious effects of the fungi and their spores when using spalted timbers.

**IN CASE OF POISONING**

**In cases of poisoning always seek professional help.**

It will be important to know which plant is responsible so whenever possible take a sample with you. Even a single red berry rules out plants with black berries but it is a greater help if you can take some leaves, flowers, seed pods etc. Put them in a plastic bag to keep them fresh, and wash your hands very thoroughly. Do not panic – there are not many plants that are seriously dangerous although a lot will cause vomiting etc.

**DISCLAIMER**

The contents of this book are provided for general information only and not for the purposes of identifying plants or medical conditions or for self-treatment. It is not a substitute for professional medical advice or services, which should always be sought whenever users of this book are concerned about their health. It is believed that the contents of this book were accurate at the time of publication but is provided 'as if' and 'with all faults'; the author and publisher is not liable for any consequential, incidental, indirect, special or other damages. It is the responsibility of the reader to verify any information given before acting upon it in any way.

## THE POISONS

There are many compounds and groups of compounds to be found in plants that can have a direct action on the health of people, their pets and their farm livestock, for better or for worse. Listed below are those that you will encounter in this book, followed by the English names of examples of the plants concerned.

**Alkaloids** - compounds encountered regularly in toxic plants and have a nitrogen molecule which causes them to be powerfully active and so in this category are such familiar substances as morphine, atropine, nicotine, quinine and strychnine. The group is subdivided and not all divisions are represented as the prime toxin in this book but some examples are as follows,

**Isoquinoline** alkaloids (Snowberry)
**Piperidine** alkaloids (Hemlock)
**Pyrrolizidine** alkaloids (Groundsel, Ragwort)
**Quinolizidine** alkaloids (Broom, Laburnum)
**Quinolone** alkaloids (Skimmia)
**Steroidal** alkaloids (Box)
**Terpenoid** alkaloids (Tansy)
**Tricyclic** alkaloids (Autumn Crocus)

Alkaloids are organic basic substances with a bitter taste, as in Daffodil, Delphinium, Hemlock, Holly, Monkshood and Snowdrops. They are usually irritating to the gastrointestinal tract producing nausea, colic and diarrhoea and also act on the central nervous system, often affecting the heart and breathing, to the point of death.

**Anthraquinones** - have an irritant laxative effect on the large intestine, causing contractions of the intestinal walls and stimulating bowel movement (Alder Buckthorn)

**Bitters -** a varied group of plants linked only by their bitter taste that stimulates secretions by the salivary glands and digestive organs. Such secretions improve the appetite and strengthen the overall function of the digestive system. Improved digestion and absorption of nutrients nourishes and strengthens the body.

**Coumarins** - a group of toxic, fragrant, organic compounds found in many plant species, all having different uses. (Sweet Vernel Grass)

**Flavonoids** are glycosides which are found widely through the vascular plant kingdom and are found distributed throughout their host. They are often the pigments that give the plant world its amazing range of colours but all in all they make up a significant percentage of plant matter, apart from water; for example, they make up nearly a third of the weight of a packet of tea. When consumed they are antioxidant which we hear about more and more in food science as we continue to discover the value of these compounds to our health: they help us fight off allergies, bacteria, inflammation and viruses and increasingly we are realising their importance in an even greater range of problems from cataracts to cancer, liver disease to asthma and in maintaining effective blood circulation. Flavonoids are divided into fourteen major classes and those into groups, such as:-

**Anthocyanins** - a large group of 260 compounds. They are the most important range of pigments after the green chlorophyll. They are familiar to gardeners for causing Hydrangeas to produce red flowers in acid soils and blue flowers in alkaline soils. All of us encounter those from fruit since they can be added to food products to adjust the colour and are used also in wines and beverages. If the sugar molecule is removed from the anthocyanin glycoside then the active part left is **anthocyanidin**.
**Chalcones** - are being explored for cancer treatment since their toxicity inhibits tumour growth.
**Flavone** - found largely in herbaceous plants, such as celery and parsley but most noticeable as yellow pigment, such as in Primroses. About 650 flavones are known.
**Flavonol** - found largely in trees and shrubs. The three most commonest are quercetin, kaempferol and myricetin. (Woodspurge)
**Isoflavonoids -** restricted largely to the legumes (peas and beans family)

**Fungi** can produce their own toxins and when they are using plants as a host they appear to make the plant poisonous. These are not usually the 'toadstool' types of fungi but those that produce minute strands, that we call moulds, mildews etc. They have serious implications for agriculture. (Blackberries, Clovers)

**Glycosides** are molecules with at least one sugar molecule which is attached to another molecule by oxygen. That other molecule is often nitrogen and this can cause toxicity if it gets released as when the sugar molecule is removed by digestion. When the sugar molecule is glucose then the glycoside is defined as a **glucoside** (Arum, Privet). It is the glucosides found in Mustard Oil, from plants belonging to the Mustard family, which cause the powerful reaction and severe gastroenteritis with purging. Mustard Oil gets its name from its colour not the plant. (Bluebell, Clematis, False Acacia, Foxgloves, Hellebores, Holly, Iris, Lily of the Valley, Oleander, White Byrony, Wood Anemone). Among the worst glucosides are those leading to cyanide, which are known as cyanogenic glucosides.

**Cardiac glycosides** - have a strong, direct action on the heart, like digitoxin, digoxin and gitoxin, helping to support its strength and rate of contraction when it falls. They are also significantly diuretic to help transfer fluids from the tissues and circulatory system to the urinary tract, thereby lowering blood pressure.

**Cyanagenic glycosides** / **Cyanagenic glucosides**- are based on that famous poison, cyanide, but in small doses they have a helpful sedative and relaxant effect on the heart and muscles. These glycosides are not poisonous in themselves but when they mix with certain enzymes during digestion they hydrolise and produce hydrocyanic acid (HCN) which is highly toxic. The effect is to starve the body of oxygen and so death can result within minutes. (Fruit, Cherry Laurel, Clover, Columbine, Trefoils). In this connection readers may also encounter **Hydrocyanic Acid** (Elder).

**Glucosilinates** - are found exclusively in species of brassicas and have an irritant effect on the skin, causing inflammation and blistering but if applied to painful and aching joints they increase blood flow to the affected area, helping to remove the build-up of waste products. It is these compounds that put the 'hot' taste into mustard and horse-radish and are believed to be the plant's deterrent against being eaten. When the material is broken up during chewing and digestion it releases isothiocyanates.

**Glycosinolates** are formed from amino acids and are found in a variety of plants, especially those of the Cabbage family and also in some cereals, such as Barley and Millet. High levels interfere with the workings of the thyroid gland, resulting in the body getting insufficient iodine and selenium. Low levels may help to safeguard against cancer.

**Isothiocyanates** result from the digestion of glycosinolates and they can interfere with the production of thyroid hormones. They do however inhibit the multiplication of cancer cells. Isothiocyanates are metabolites of cyanide but do not themselves contain cyanide and nor do they have the same poisoning effects. They give the distinctive flavour to Broccoli and other brassicas.

**Lectins** are proteins that have the potential to damage the intestines, making them poisonous in themselves but their action makes them anti-nutritional, leading to deficiency conditions etc. We encounter lectins most often in beans but they are responsible for the toxicity of Tulips.

**Nitrate** poisoning is actually **nitrite** poisoning. It occurs when fodder is rich in nitrates, which, during digestion, are reduced to nitrites. When these are absorbed into the bloodstream they react with the oxygen-carrying haemoglobin to form methaemoglobin which is incapable of releasing oxygen and that can prove fatal in minutes. (Rape, Brassicas)

**Oxalic acid / oxalates** - calcium oxalate and potassium oxalate are soluble in water (and therefore blood) but in sufficient amounts can cause the precipitation of calcium into calcium oxalate crystals which are insoluble, causing hypocalcemia in the blood and acute kidney failure due to calcium oxalate crystals blocking the renal tubules. Smaller quantities of calcium oxalate thicken the blood by coagulation. (Black Bryony, Docks, Fat Hen, Good King Henry, Rhubarb, Sorrel, Spinach, Wood Sorrel)

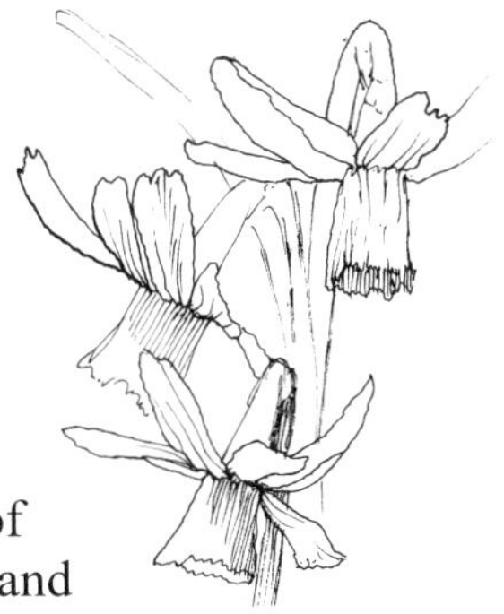

**Phenols** - a group of compounds found in many plants and includes salicylic acid of aspirin fame. They are also antiseptic and reduce inflammation when taken internally. See also tannins.

**Potassium Oxalate** – as per calcium oxalate.

**Saponins** are glycosides that upset the digestive system violently, causing vomiting and diarrhoea. If they get into the bloodstream they cause a breakdown of red blood cells and so injure the central nervous system producing convulsions and paralysis. (Ivy, Butchers Broom, Dogs Mercury, Fat Hen, Snowberry, Herb Paris). There are two main types.

> **Steroidal saponins** are found widely in plants and have a distinctly hormonal effect, having similarities with the steroid hormones produced naturally in the body.
> **Triterpenoid saponins** are often strongly expectorant but may be useful in the absorption of nutrients.

**Tannins** – are found in most of the green vascular plants and can cause problems when found in large amounts, as in forage legumes. Avoid consuming large amounts of any plant known to have high concentrations of tannins since these precipitate proteins, causing irritation to the digestive system from stomach to bowel, plus liver damage. Tannins are implicated in certain types of cancer while on the other hand they contract the tissues of the body, which improves resistance to infection.

**Thiaminase** interferes with the production of thiamine (vitamin $B_1$) which is needed for the metabolism of carbohydrate. Such deficiency affects the brain and nervous system plus the heart and vascular system, and is best known as the forms of beriberi diseases. Problems will also arise when the body actually needs more than its usual level of thiamine, either due to other illnesses, such as liver disease, or simply during pregnancy and lactation. Severe cases can lead to blindness and death (Bracken, Horsetails, Male Fern)

**Tropanes** interfere with the transmission of impulses from nerve cell to nerve cell and can therefore stop the body working in a very short space of time. With skilful, controlled use they are among the world's most important drugs, from atropine and scopolamine to hyoscyamine. They can therefore play an important part in the control or treatment of major problems such as Parkinson's Disease. (Deadly Nightshade, Henbane, Potato, Thorn apple).

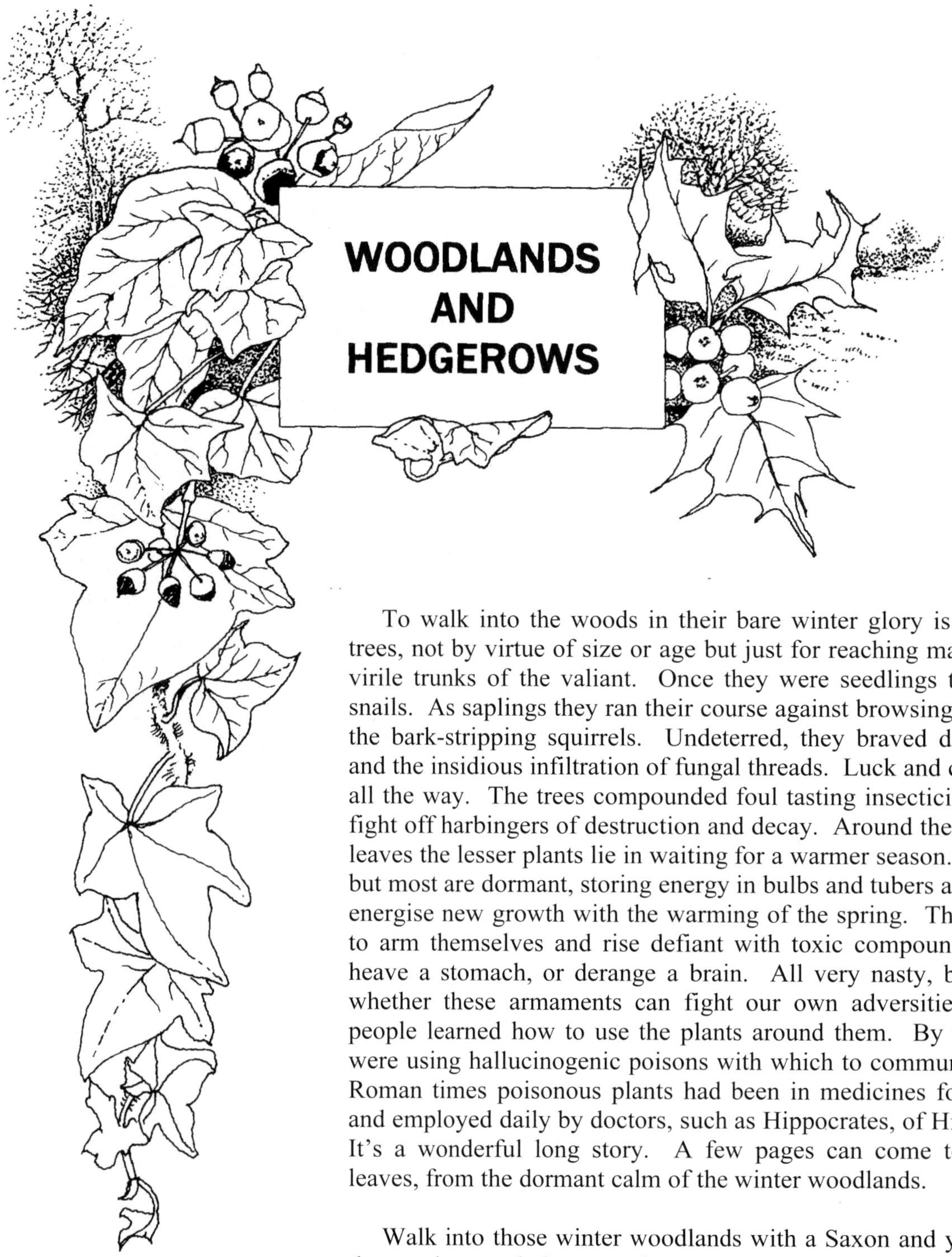

# WOODLANDS AND HEDGEROWS

To walk into the woods in their bare winter glory is to see the champion trees, not by virtue of size or age but just for reaching maturity. These are the virile trunks of the valiant. Once they were seedlings that eluded slugs and snails. As saplings they ran their course against browsing rabbits and deer, and the bark-stripping squirrels. Undeterred, they braved defoliating caterpillars and the insidious infiltration of fungal threads. Luck and chemistry rode pillion all the way. The trees compounded foul tasting insecticides and fungicides to fight off harbingers of destruction and decay. Around their feet amid the fallen leaves the lesser plants lie in waiting for a warmer season. A few are evergreen but most are dormant, storing energy in bulbs and tubers and rhizomes, ready to energise new growth with the warming of the spring. Then they too will need to arm themselves and rise defiant with toxic compounds, to burn a mouth, heave a stomach, or derange a brain. All very nasty, but pause and ponder whether these armaments can fight our own adversities. Even Stone Age people learned how to use the plants around them. By the Bronze Age they were using hallucinogenic poisons with which to commune with the gods. By Roman times poisonous plants had been in medicines for thousands of years and employed daily by doctors, such as Hippocrates, of Hippocratic Oath fame. It's a wonderful long story. A few pages can come to life, like unfurling leaves, from the dormant calm of the winter woodlands.

Walk into those winter woodlands with a Saxon and you might have heard the word *cneowholen*, meaning **Holly** (*Ilex aquifolium* L.) that is knee-high. It may have been descriptive but it may also have been a term of specific importance, a measurement used in agreements and in the courts when there were disagreements. They probably coppiced the Holly at regular intervals, when it was knee-high, and the winter would have been the time. This was the season of frugal living, for both man and beast, and the survival and the prosperity of the community depended upon getting their livestock through to spring. Hay was the prime winter feed and the skill of making it was hundreds of years old when the Saxons arrived with it, only to find that the native Romano-British were hay-making already. Hay is not entirely nutritious though. The livestock benefited a dietary supplement of fresh greens. The Saxon landscape was short of those when the frost curtailed grazing but in the woodlands there were Holly trees. The tufts of knee-high new growth would have been ideal since the stems had yet to lengthen and so were still thick-set with leaves. The frosts encouraged the wood to harden and so it took several

blows of the bill-hook to sever the stems. Oh yes they soon got warm doing that but what a back-breaking job. No doubt they learned to drape sackcloth across their shoulders as extra protection against the prickly leaves before they backpacked the harvest home. Of course the Holly arms itself against being eaten by growing prickly leaves but these are not a sure guarantee. The livestock would have nibbled slowly and carefully but there wasn't anything else to enjoy or even to do, so it reduced problems arising from winter boredom. However, the Holly is armed with toxins. When consumed in small doses, as in a dietary supplement, they do not seem to harm livestock. Indeed it perks them up; a little bit of poison is liable to jolt the digestive system into greater action. Not all scientists are in agreement over the toxicity of Holly. It does contain a bitter glycoside called ilicin but some scientists believe that the symptoms of poisoning result from the presence of two alkaloids, called methylxanthines. They are caffeine and theobromine, as in tea, coffee and chocolate (A species of Holly is used for tea in South America). They give the bitter flavouring and are mild stimulants - in the human central nervous system theobromine has its slightly anti-depressant action by raising levels of serotonin. It's a rare compound, found in only about sixty of the world's plants. Used wisely it acts as a mild diuretic by stimulating the kidneys and so reduces any build up of fluids in the body, resulting from a heart condition. Better still, it can be mixed with medication derived from Foxgloves to reduce conditions such as high blood pressure; and it relaxes the smooth muscles of the bronchi in the lungs, to help alleviate respiratory problems. While medical sciences have been reaching these levels of understanding stockman have been quietly continuing the practice of gathering it for winter feed, right up to within living memory. In the Welsh *Mabinogion* is the account of the *Dream of Rhonabwy* which in its surviving written form is thought to date from the 13th century and therein we can enter one of those homes where man and beast shared the same roof:

*"And as they came towards the house, they could see a black old hall with a straight gable end, and smoke a-plenty from it. And when they came inside, they could see a floor full of holes and uneven. Where there was a bump upon it, it was with difficulty that a man might stand thereon, so exceedingly slippery was the floor with cows' urine and dung, and branches of holly a-plenty on the floor after the cattle had eaten off their tips."*

(*The Mabinogion*, trans. G. Jones and T. Jones. 1949)

Our ancestors not only gathered Holly as winter fodder but also that other evergreen, the **Ivy** (*Hedera helix* L.). No doubt that put some flavour into the boring daily ration of hay. The toxins would have given a bit of a jolt to the digestive system but animals can consume it safely in small amounts, whether wild animals like deer or domestic animals like feral ponies and cattle in the New Forest. A few old photographs show shepherds feeding Ivy to their flock. We see them handing it out. Maybe this was a rationing stratagem to control the risk of poisoning or maybe it was just a demonstration for the photographer. Today we see more Ivy growing up the roadside and hedgerow trees than our ancestors ever did. Look at the great landscape paintings by artists, such as John Constable, and the ivy-clad trees are missing; they do not appear on medieval illuminated pages either. Trees were too valuable to be left to the ravages of Ivy. It was kept in check by regular harvesting for winter fodder and by the regular gatherings throughout the year for ritual usage. In pre-Reformation times, greenery such as Ivy was used for decorating churches and other buildings on holy days; Ivy was associated with the Virgin Mary. To get all this, they would have sought it out on the shady side of hedge-banks and across the woodland floor. The plant has adaptations that give it great shade-tolerance and so today we find it as the last survivor when trees shade out the rest of the ground flora - a sure indicator that the woodland is young. This would have happened in the coppiced woodlands as the crop matured towards the end of the cycle. It is one of the reasons the wild animals turn to woodland browsing in hard weather and why man turned his beasts out there too.

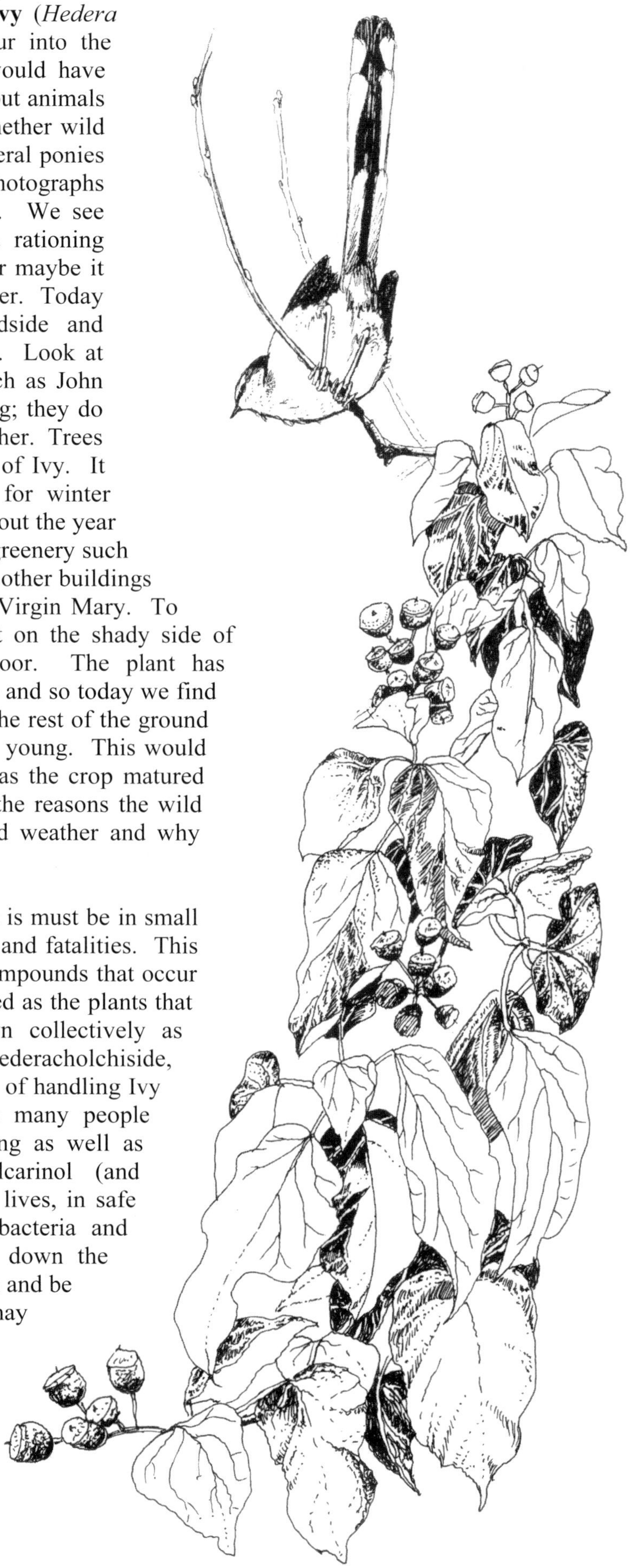

The crucial point about ivy-fodder is that is must be in small amounts or else it soon produces poisoning and fatalities. This is most likely due to saponins, which are compounds that occur widely in the plant kingdom and are as varied as the plants that produce them. Those of Ivy are known collectively as hederasaponins or just hederin, and one, hederacholchiside, has been used in cancer treatments. Beware of handling Ivy too much with bare hands since it gives many people dermatitis, sometimes severe, with blistering as well as inflammation. This is caused by falcarinol (and didehydrofalcarinol), which also enters our lives, in safe amounts, in carrots. It helps fight off bacteria and research in Denmark found that it slows down the growth of cancer cells. It may also ease pain and be slightly sedative. Some of the toxicity may arise when the foliage is damaged (as in handling or chewing), because compounds mix together that had been kept separate by the plant. Certainly beware of inhaling the vapours that result if the stuff is put through a shredder. These can cause coughing and headaches which should be warning enough. The active compounds have of course attracted herbalists who have used Ivy in their treatments for such diverse problems as abscesses, boils, bronchitis, burns, chilblains, coughs, dropsy, drunkenness, dysentery, evil spirits, fevers, gum disease, headache, mouth ulcers, mumps, neuralgia, plague, rheumatism, scalds, sores, sore throats, sunburn, toothache and whooping cough. That does not mean the medicines were either safe or effective. Never try using Ivy in home-made recipes as it has such a complicated mix of compounds that it is crucial not to overdose on some of them. For example, in small amounts Ivy can cause blood vessels to dilate while in higher doses it causes them to constrict – too far either way could be lethal.

Turning to that low clumper, the **Butcher's Broom** (*Ruscus aculeatus* L.), we are not at much risk nowadays as we have stopped using the young shoots as a substitute for Asparagus, to which it is related. It's weird. The flattened spear-heads that look like leaves are in fact modified stems (cladodes) and are very hard and sharply-pointed. It looks most unappetising, inspiring Hulme's observation that it looks '*about as tempting a delicacy as scrap-iron.*' Bunches were used for scouring butchers' blocks but today its main market is with the florists, especially in early autumn when it bears bright scarlet berries, the size of a small cherry. Those can tempt children to eat them, especially as they are sweet but they soon turn bitter, causing vomiting and then diarrhoea, so the toxins are soon voided. They are steroidal saponins, including ruscogenin, but not enough to make the plant highly toxic. Large consumptions are said to lead to convulsions but there are no reported cases of severe poisoning from Britain. Don't be the first. Its compounds are used in medicines, being added to some Horse Chestnut Extract products for example, taken as treatment for varicose veins to increase the elasticity of the veins and thereby the function of their valves. It should be taken only under qualified medical supervision due to its toxic action.

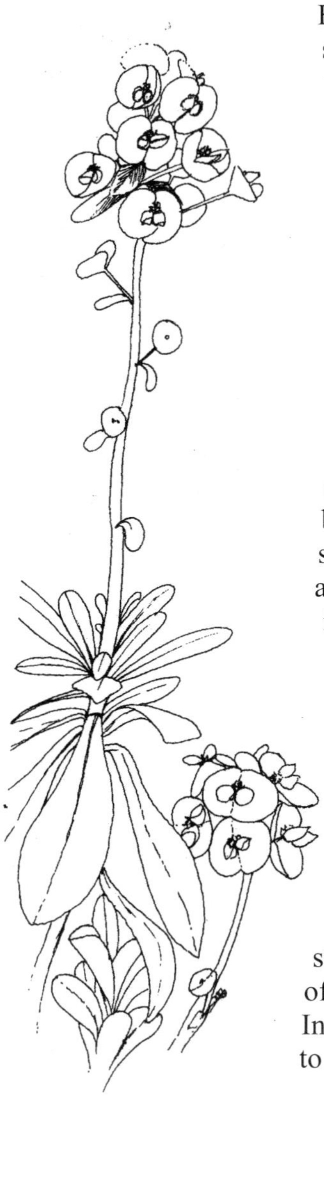

Also remaining evergreen, or partially so, is the **Wood Spurge** (*Euphorbia amygdaloides* L.) which belongs to a very large genus of some 2000 species. Eighteen are found wild in Britain, plus subspecies and a wider range in gardens, and Wood Spurge is one of the eight Euphorbias that vets have to deal with most often. All have a white latex sap which is caustic and irritant. Do not get this smeared into your eyes, let alone eat it. Apparently it tastes bitter and burns the mouth and digestive tract, causing vomiting and diarrhoea. Persevere with eating this stuff and the next phase of symptoms sounds highly unpleasant, with seething pain backwards and forwards through the head. There seems to be no part of the body that it does not affect and it produces some odd sensations too, like the illusion of a smell of mice. Keep it out of hay too, since drying does not destroy the toxins. They are believed to be flavonol glycosides but the plant is not fully understood yet and nor is it known how much is likely to be a fatal dose.

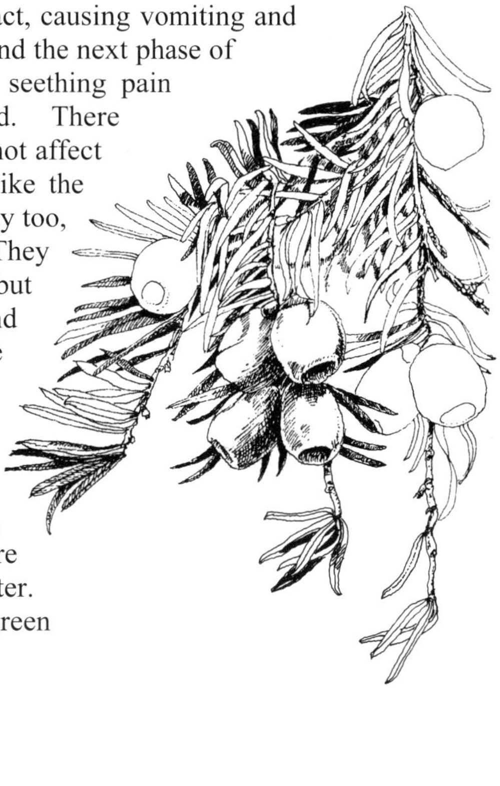

Only four plants so far and already the winter woodlands are much more interesting places. There are a few rarities, such as the *Daphne* species but they're more often found in the garden and are in that chapter. In the woodlands there is still one major evergreen to consider and that's the famous Yew.

**Yew** (*Taxus baccata* L.) is one of our best known and much loved trees, from the ancient specimens in churchyards to the romantic notion of a 'Druid grove' out in our woodlands. The tree has stunning powers of self-protection and regeneration, so that seven specimens in Britain are reckoned to be over 4,000 years old, including the one in the churchyard at Crowhurst, Surrey, of which three bole portraits illustrate these pages. It has a different profile from every angle! The hollow has been used as a meeting room, hence the provision of a door. Such trees were alive at the beginning of the Bronze Age. Another eight might be over 3,000 years old and so were growing when the first villages evolved. They have stirred the minds of those communities ever since, featuring in the old pagan faiths and passing into Christianity as the sacred tree of churchyards, primarily in England, particularly Eastern and Southern England.

Do you know, if you sleep under a Yew tree you'll see the Prince of Fairyland and his entire retinue ride by? That's according to one of the folk beliefs relating to its mind-altering powers. Today, some people say they get a "funny feeling" if they linger among Yews and one family related how it makes the placid father become bad tempered all the time he's by one. He can't control it and calms down immediately upon leaving the tree's presence. It has powerful narcotic compounds. No wonder Yews have been employed all around the world, for health and longevity of the body and in funeral rituals for the good of the soul.

Those powerful compounds are well known for being dangerously toxic to livestock. A well-known explanation for Yews in churchyards has them growing there to separate them separate from the village animals. This is false. Medieval churchyards were grazed regularly. Sometimes the animals were owned by the priest; sometimes they were owned by the church itself to raise income; and sometimes the parish leased out the grazing to save cutting the grass. The Yews are there for ritual reasons rather than practical. It is true, however, that eating Yew can result in sudden death. The tree holds a mixture of powerful alkaloids (known collectively as taxin or taxine), which are absorbed rapidly into the bloodstream and then interrupt the action of the heart. The toxins do not degenerate with drying, but are concentrated, so hedge-clippings abandoned beside pastures are a major hazard. Interestingly, studies made by Southampton University found that feral livestock in the New Forest took mouthfuls of Yew, by choice, every day. Horses are normally very susceptible but the New Forest ponies are a very old breed with a tough genetic make-up to enable them to cope with rough grazing. Some of that capacity has been lost in the selective breeding that gives us modern thoroughbred horses. Yew trees vary in their toxicity too. Nevertheless, best practice is to keep livestock well away from Yews and even if the green foliage is out of reach beware of the brown fallen needles that might be grazed up. Humans are more likely to eat the beautiful red fruits which are so well-known for being poisonous that they have not caused too much of a problem. Now the situation is changing. Modern analytical studies are revealing that although the central seed in the fruit is highly toxic the red flesh round it has very low toxicity. Consequently people have started eating the red flesh and spitting out the seed. Such acts of bravado are all very well but 'low' toxicity does not mean 'completely safe.' These are cardiac toxins so anybody with a heart condition should certainly think twice. Remember too that Yew trees vary in their degree of toxicity; they have not been bred to uniformity like domesticated fruit trees. Similarly, people vary in their levels of tolerance to the compounds. The wise will leave Yew berries well alone.

In the second half of the 20th century Yews hit international headlines for yielding an anti-cancer drug. It was then called taxol but now TAXOL® is a registered trade name of Bristol-Myers Squibb and we need to get our tongues round paclitaxel for general usage. The story starts in 1958 when the United States National Cancer Institute decided to screen 35,000 plants for anti-cancer compounds. That was a very ambitious programme so it was 1963 before it was the turn of the Yew and the United States Forest Service sent in samples from the Pacific Yew, *Taxus brevifolia*. In 1971 an active ingredient (to be known as compound 17) was discovered in the bark by Dr Monroe Wall and Dr Mansukh Wani working for the Research Triangle Institute in North Carolina. This became the famous paclitaxel, which kills cancer cells in a way previously unknown. Initially it was rejected, due to extraction and production problems. Interest was revived in 1979 when Dr Susan Band Horwitz of the Albert Einstein College of Medicine in New York asked for a sample of the new compound and started investigating it. It was she who appreciated how odd was the convoluted molecular structure of the compound, so odd that she said no scientist would have imagined engineering it. Then she found that its action in a cancer cell was unique: it halts some of the workings of the cell so that the cell cannot reproduce but remains 'frozen' for the rest of its life span and then simply dies. The trouble is, the Yew trees die too, from having their bark stripped off. It takes the bark of six trees, each over a hundred years old, to produce enough paclitaxel to treat just one patient. A renewable resource needed to be found.

In France the research was taken up by Pierre Potier of the Chemical Institute of Natural Substances, where he and his colleagues had been searching since 1968 for new substances that could be developed as anti-cancer drugs. They developed a new simple biological test, known as the 'tubulin test' to help them screen out promising compounds (microtubules are the part of the cell structure that are prevented from functioning by compounds like palcitaxel). Thus they found in the Yew's foliage a precursor of paclitaxel that became known as 'baccatin' and during their biosynthesis of this they discovered a compound that reacts positively to their tubulin test. It's twice as active as paclitaxel and was registered as TAXOTERE® and is now prescribed throughout the world. It has saved the Yew trees because the pharmaceutical companies no longer need to strip the bark. They can use the foliage and can get supplies of greenery from anyone and everyone who has a Yew hedge and is prepared to save the clippings and have them collected (contact Limehurst Ltd, Chichester or Yew Clippings Ltd, Bridport).

The next stage was to synthesise the compound in a laboratory without any greenery at all and the first report of that appeared in 1994 (*Journal of the American Chemical Society*). Twenty years on and hundreds of thousands of patients all around the world have been treated with these drugs. They are not effective for *all* cancers but excel for some of the major ones, like ovarian and breast cancers. Some patients develop a resistance to the drugs and Susan Horwitz has moved on towards trying to defeat this problem and has two promising compounds. One, epothilone, was found in South African soil bacteria and the other, discodermolide, comes from a Caribbean sea sponge.

Twelfth Night comes and goes, followed by Distaff Sunday and then on Plough Monday the men return to work. On their way out to the scoured fields they pass fresh signs of the new season they shall be working towards. In the woods and sheltered hedge banks new growth begins to spring. The **Wild Arum** (*Arum maculatum* L.) spears up very early. It's luscious brilliant green leaves that must be so tempting to herbivores and to our ancestors seeking fresh greens for the cooking pot. It has an astonishing total of some hundred English names including Cuckoo Pint and Lords-and-Ladies, with some of the names being of Saxon origin, which testifies to the continuous need to talk about this plant. Children were sent out to find it because it was of practical value. Children were also instructed to leave it alone because it is highly charged with toxins, proven killers of children. It grows from small tubers which contain starch and lathering agents called saponins. These were dug up and used for laundering clothing. The use of starch for this purpose was introduced into England from the Continent in the 16th century and led to the extravagant starched collars and cuffs of the Elizabethan and Stuart fashions. Various vegetable starches were used: Wheat for general purposes, Bluebell and Daffodil bulbs for that little bit extra, but Arum was best of all. In 1597 John Gerard wrote

"*The most pure and white starch is made from the roots of the cuckow-pint; but most hurtful to the hands of the laundresses that hath the handling of it, for it choppeth, blistereth, and maketh rough and rugged and withal smarting.*"

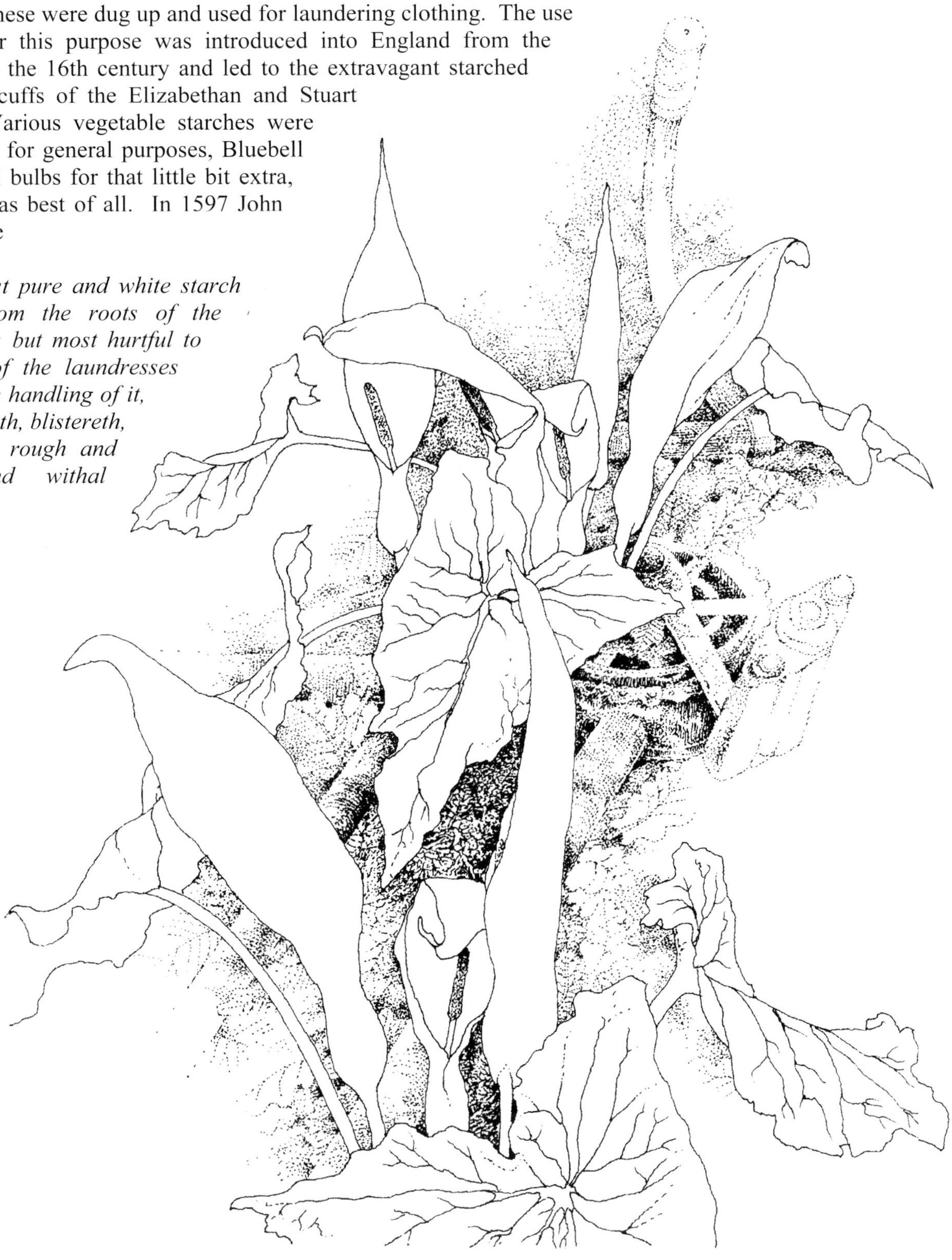

Consequently it is said that when seeking a new laundry girl at the mop fairs, the girl with the worst hands was hired since she obviously had the most experience! The inflammation was due in no small part to the compound aronine which is caustic to the skin (and savage to soft internal tissue if swallowed). Part of the reaction was due to the needle-like crystals of calcium oxalate and there are potassium salts in the plant too, just as in Wood Sorrel. Despite all these toxins, our ancestors discovered how to process the tuber starch to produce a safe food: Portland sago/Portland arrow root, used in blancmanges etc. Arum species are still used for food in countries like Turkey, India and Bangladesh. In 18th century Paris there was a cosmetic called Cyprus powder which was said to contain starch from this plant. The Italians have used the tuber sap to try and remove freckles and other blemishes but it is liable to cause blistering at the least.

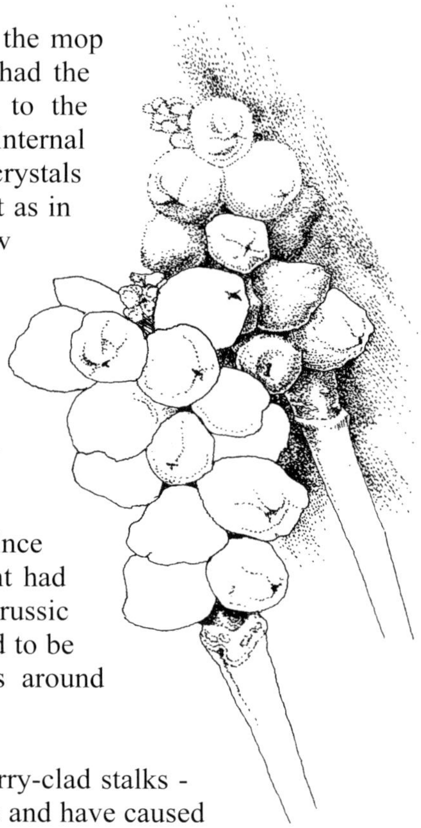

Arum's rising foliage looks luscious but do not be tempted, since bruising enables various compounds to mix together which the plant had kept separate. These are cyanophoric glucosides, which produce prussic acid (cyanide), so don't eat them, even though it is said that they used to be added to the cooking pot. More to the point, check hedgerows around pastures to safeguard livestock.

The leaves die down straight after flowering, leaving only the berry-clad stalks - green at first but turning to brilliant glossy red. They are highly toxic and have caused deaths in children. When it comes to learning which plants to avoid make sure this one is high on the priority list, especially as it is so common. Apart from woodlands and hedgerows it occurs in shady gardens, where some of its relatives are grown too (e.g. *Arum pictum*). All should be left well alone. Fortunately children who eat them are usually halted by a strong burning sensation in the mouth and throat but obviously this hasn't always been a sufficient deterrent. Presumably they have been swallowed whole.

In complete contrast to the bold dark green arrow-head leaves of the Wild Arum are the little soft green trefoils of the **Wood Sorrel** (*Oxalis acetosella* L.). They too come up early in the year, putting pale patches on the moist-dark mould. Soon they are over-topped by silent little white bells that swing up and open wide in any welcome stirring of sunshine. These plants were much sought after. In the mouth they are vinegar-sharp but our ancestors liked strong flavours and after a winter with little but a hint of leek and onion in the bland gruels they were very welcome. Bunches of leaves were sunk into the cooking pot and possibly some were eaten fresh with the bread but it is not clear to what extent our medieval ancestors ate fresh fruit and salad leaves. They obviously learned at some early date that Wood Sorrel is toxic in large amounts. They used it carefully, not so much as a pot herb but as the prime flavouring in their 'spring sauce' or 'green sauce' (oxalis comes from the Greek for sour). The sharp taste was due to toxic compounds but in small amounts they gave a bit of a jolt to the digestive system that was not only debilitated after the long winter of poor repetitive rations but was now suffering the deprivations of the long Lenten fast running up to Easter. That was the period when the Church dropped the jubilant Alleluia from the services as it prepared to mourn Christ's death. It was re-introduced on Easter Day to celebrate the Resurrection and the Wood Sorrel was believed to burst into bloom to celebrate as well and so got called Alleluia.

Well that's what William Turner wrote but in 1568 but that was after the Reformation and is a retrospective view. The explanation doesn't take into account that Easter is a moveable Feast up and down the calendar and therefore flowering would not always coincide, let alone in France and Italy where the plant also got this name. It is more likely that this tangy herb was frowned upon by the Catholic Church as an inappropriate pleasure during Lent. They could enjoy it again on Easter Day – Alleluia! They couldn't get enough of it, by relying on the market traders proffering their bunches, and so from at least the 14th century it was cultivated in the herb gardens. Of course they did not love it just for the taste. They could feel it doing them good. It was a rich source of much-needed vitamin C and had compounds that jollied up the digestive system so that they could both enjoy and benefit from the richer food of the Easter Feast. Those compounds include oxalic acid and potassium oxalate. Eat too much of those and a corrosive action burns its way from mouth to stomach, causing vomiting, but it could be too late by then. Muscular tremors set in, followed by convulsions, collapse and death. Some people have died within a few minutes while others have taken days. An apparent recovery can be misleading since crystals of calcium oxalate form and block the little tubes in the kidneys, killing the patient slowly by renal failure. Nevertheless, there have been various attempts to exploit it as a medicine, for conditions ranging from sore throats to diphtheria, acne to tumours. Today oxalic acid is used as a rust remover and in bleaches to remove iron stains. As food it is included in the 'wild food' mixture of at least one company in Britain. Otherwise we simply concur with Gertrude Jekyll that it is the "tenderest and loveliest" of woodland plants.

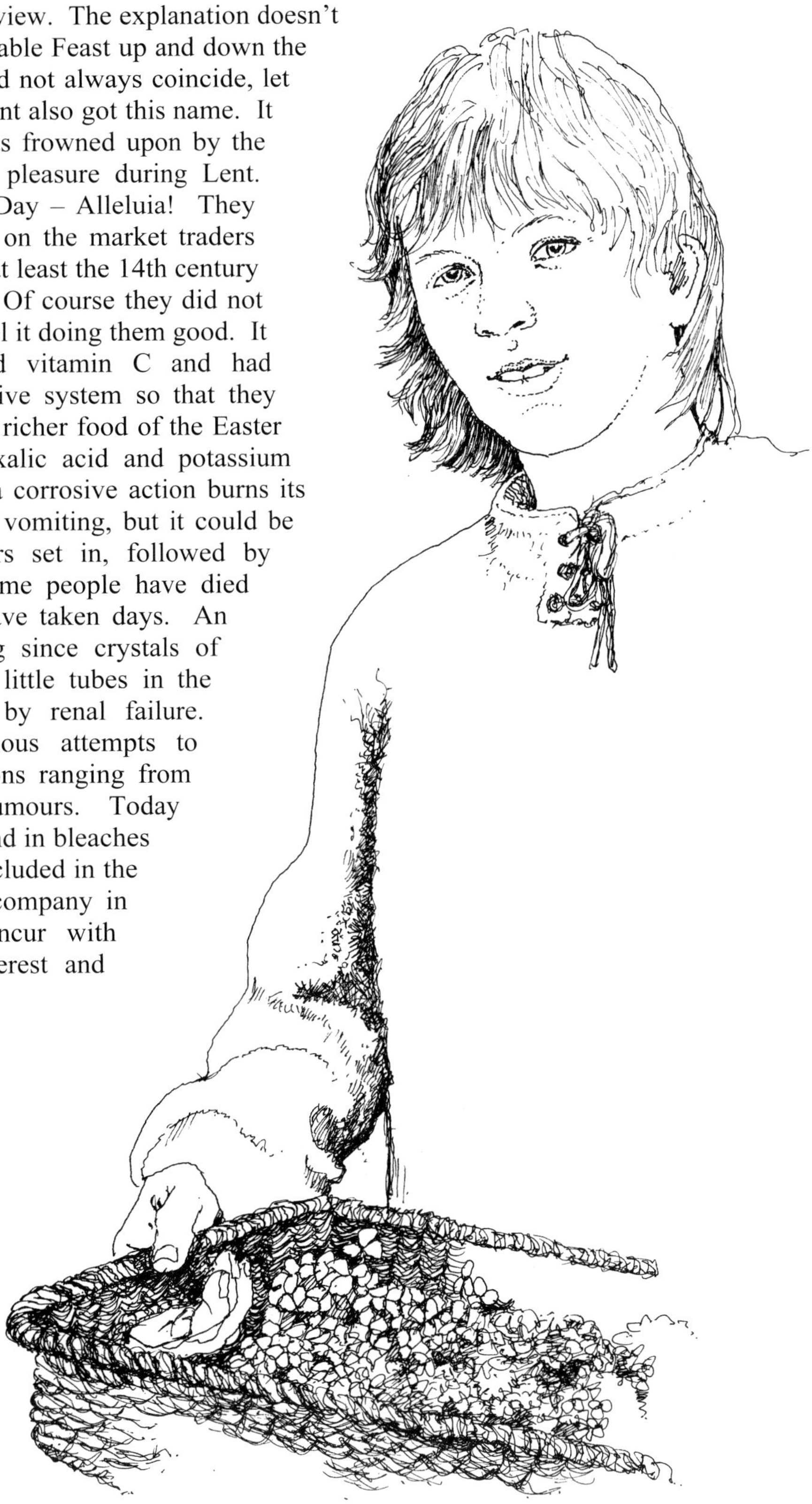

The first few hours of bright sunshine make the **Wood Anemone** (*Anemone nemorosa* L.) turn up its white bells, to open flat and show off the dome of golden stamens in a haze of delicate scent. Carpets of them can grace the coppiced woodlands and are therefore one of the ancient scenes of an English spring but our ancestors failed to put them to much use. They tried it for treating all sorts of sores but soon found it was too caustic. For other complaints people were recommended to chew the root but only because spitting was considered so efficacious!

Animals avoid it too because Wood Anemones belong to the buttercup family, Ranunculaceae, that produces the glycoside ranunculin, which is very toxic to mammals. Damaging the foliage, by chewing it, releases enzymes that change the ranunculin into a highly irritant volatile oil, called protoanemonine. This compound is unstable and changes again, into anemonine, and that is non-toxic. By then though, the caustic stage may already have caused severe irritation and blistering. It's rendered harmless by drying but it is not likely to end up in hay. Boiling makes it safe too but by then so much of the other nutrition has been destroyed. So our ancestors simply left it alone, to please the mind with its beauty.

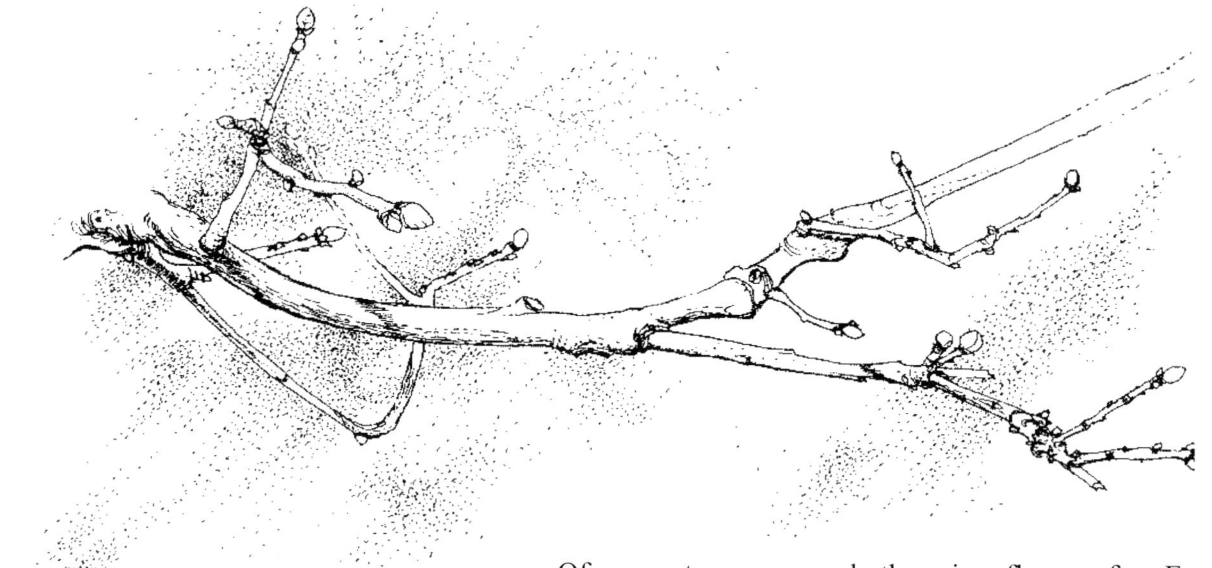

Of course to many people the prime flower of an English spring is the richly scented **Bluebell** (*Hyacinthoides non-scripta L.*). It was dedicated to St. George (once he had supplanted St. Michael as patron saint of England) since people noticed they came into bloom by his saint's day, 23rd April. This became more reliable after the calendar was changed by eleven days in 1752. It is a very English flower, which in other countries does not usually produce the extensive carpets of bloom that we have always taken for granted as one of the glories of an English spring. This bit of ecology must have been known to the Elizabethans since John Gerard recorded them as 'Hyacinthus Anglicus', explaining that "*it is thought to grow more plentifully in England than elsewhere.*" That has been fortunate since the plant has important practical uses. The great carpets were a lavish source of bulbs, each of which bulges with a mucilage that dries into a powerful glue. It was used by the fletchers to affix flights to arrows; just imagine how many Bluebells fought on a medieval battlefield! The bookbinders used the same for gluing pages between the covers. Gerard noted that as a laundry starch it was second best after *Arum maculatum*. He might also have pointed out that when being gathered, the greenery was torn off the bulbs and thrown away, rather than being fed to the livestock, since a symptom of poisoning was a reduction in milk yield. That was the last thing people wanted at Bluebell time when the livestock were suckling. Despite knowing this, it has taken a very long time to investigate the active compounds and so we are still learning from this plant. Currently they are described as glycosides and lumped together under the name scillaren (or transvaallin). It constricts the blood vessels and affects the heart muscles in similar ways to the glycosides that can be obtained from Foxgloves. It can therefore be valuable in restoring a disfunctioning heart. It was not until 1923 that this cardiac stimulant was finally identified and described as two compounds, scillaren A and a less pure form, scillaren B. Both are used in modern drugs but which are not exactly a substitute for the Foxglove's digitalin. Scillaren is more effective on the associated nervous system while being less dramatic on the heart muscle, so it is often preferred to digitalin in the treatment of tachycardias. Also, it acts quicker but is less persistent so there are fewer dangers from a build-up of the compound in the body. There's another toxin in Bluebells that goes under the name scilliroside and is the one that causes people to vomit if they consume the plant. Rats and other rodents cannot vomit and so it kills them. Man has exploited that as a selective and very successful rodenticide, especially as rodents are continuous feeders and soon ingest large amounts, but production worldwide of this highly toxic material was halted in 1980. The original plant source was not the Bluebell but the Red Squill, *Urginea maritima*, from the Mediterranean.

**Horsetails** (*Equisetum spp.*), of which there are twelve in Britain, growing everywhere from our woodlands to watersides. They are increasingly called Mare's-tails nowadays, although that name has traditionally been reserved for a flowering aquatic plant, *Hippuris vulgaris* L.. The Horsetails are so ancient they do not have flowers but have cones instead, as per the illustration which is of the Giant Horsetail, *Equisetum telmateia* Ehrh.. The foreground stems are drawn life-size, but many people will know lesser versions, especially if they feel their garden is cursed with them. They are indestructible. They have also been valuable. The greenery leaves your hands feeling gritty because up to 10% of the plant can be of silica compounds and can be used for abrasion, so bowyers polished their bows and fletchers polished their arrows with it, while polishing pewter gave rise to the name Pewterwort. In the mid 20th century the Dolmetsch family were polishing some of their reproduction period musical instruments with it because unlike commercial glasspaper it does not leave fine scratches. In herbal medicines it has been used to combat silica deficiency problems. Despite it being an ancient 'primitive' plant it has a surprisingly rich chemistry, including gold, which might make it useful in treating arthritis. It is already yielding compounds useful in treating some heart and kidney problems. There are disadvantages too so it is inadvisable to let children handle it excessively since ingestion of the juice off the hands is believed to cause adverse reactions. The sap contains a surprisingly high number of active compounds. Most of these have been implicated in poisoning, especially equisetine, although some scientists doubt that these in themselves cause the reported fatalities in livestock. Nevertheless, consuming Horsetails can be fatal; all livestock should be kept well away from them. The toxins are not destroyed by drying and so it has proved fatal in hay, with as little as 5% thought to be a lethal dose. Horsetails contain the dire thiaminase, which splits the molecules of thiamine (vitamin B) causing deficiency diseases, which may take two or more weeks to show up. Horses are particularly vulnerable, and soon weaken and fall.

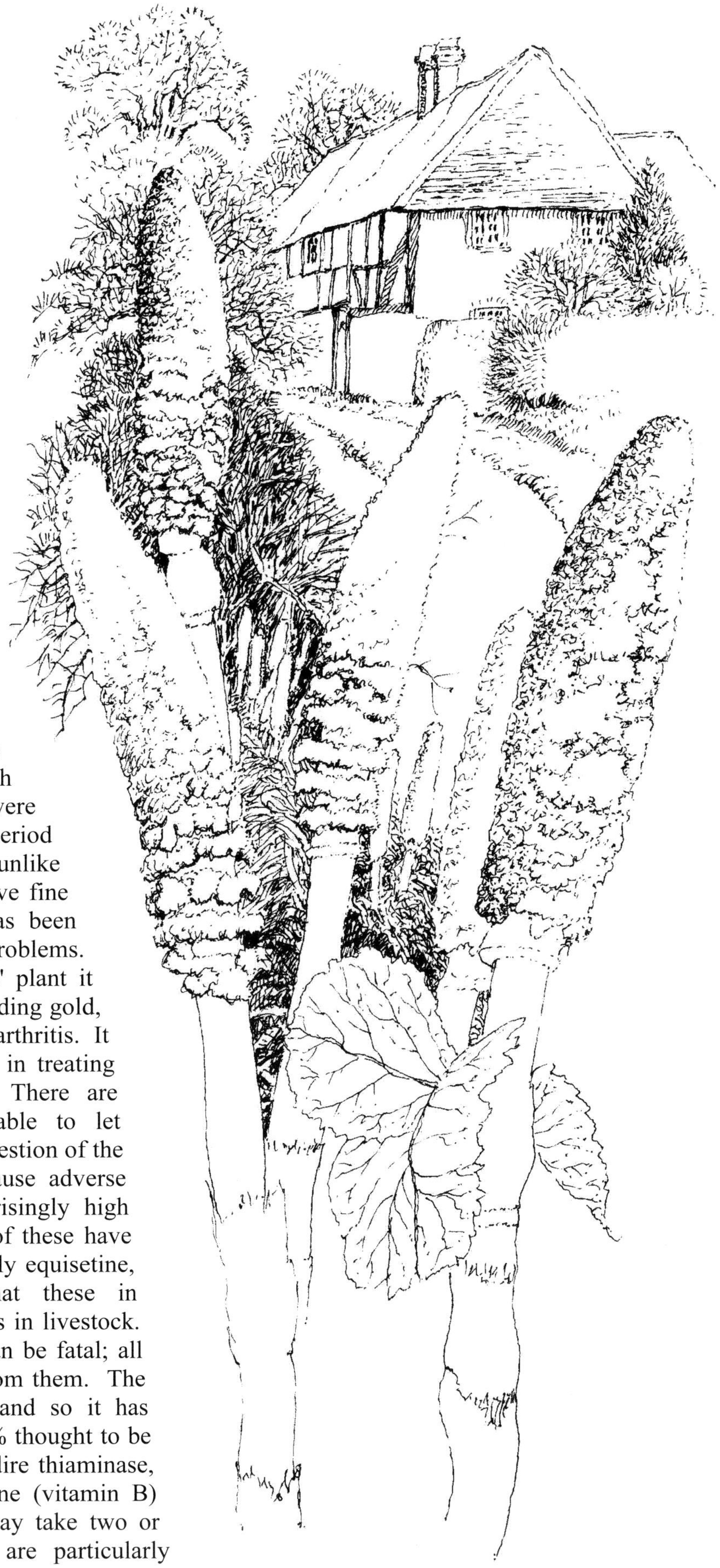

Alongside the Bluebells and Wood Anemones are the green-flowered shoots of the **Dog's Mercury** (*Mercurialis perennis* L.) which can sprout in masses across the woodland floor, especially under the Beeches of the southern chalk downs. Centuries of experience have taught that this plant should not be eaten, even after cooking, and neither should livestock be allowed to graze it. It contains noxious saponins. There is also a volatile oil which was isolated in the 19th century and named mercurialine but better known nowadays as methylamine. It's a hazardous chemical used widely in industry, for the making of such diverse products as dyes and insecticides. The plants contains trimethylamine and hermidine as well. Do not over-handle or consume the plant, or its annual relative *Mercurialis annua* L. that looks so similar (garden and arable weed), since it will cause irritation to skin, eyes, and digestive systems, producing pain, vomiting and diarrhoea, before it gets going on the liver, kidneys and heart.

Overtopping the ground flora the mature trees are coming into leaf, like the **Oaks** (*Quercus* spp.) bursting into their wonderful mustard colours and this is when the Oaks defend their buds most heavily with toxic compounds. They are intended to make them unpalatable but if cattle browse them heavily they can taint the milk. It is the acorns in the autumn that bring problems because these nutritious fruits, rich in carbohydrate, are defended by tannins. When ingested, these have an astringent action that draws fluid out of the cells and shrinks them. That is ideal for the tanning industry but not good for the health of the living animal. Potentially, acorns can be a serious cause of poisoning. They are also implicated in dermatitis and eczema. Nevertheless, there are still farmers who know just how few to use to treat any livestock with bad diarrhoea. Using too many leads to fatalities. This even applies to pigs, despite their famous history of being driven out into the medieval woods to feed on acorns. Presumably medieval pigs, being related so closely to their wild ancestors, had tougher constitutions than modern pigs, although pigs are still put to pannage in the New Forest. Wildlife in general use acorns as an important source of autumn feed and do not seem to suffer ill effects. Wood Pigeons are very fond of them. Stories of the Ancient Greeks having acorns as their staple food, before cereals were developed, refer to different species of Oak. Do not eat British acorns.

When winter shortages drive animals to scour for greenery they can be attracted by the **Male Fern** (*Dryopteris filix-mas* L. Schott) which can be semi-evergreen. In mild winters the fronds persist until they collapse in the spring to make way for fresh growth. To fuel the production of new growth the fern stores energy in large crowns at ground level and livestock seek these out. The crowns are particularly toxic. This should be no surprise since the chief use of the fern, for hundreds of years, was to rid the body of tapeworms. Louis XVI paid Madame Louffer 1800 francs to publish her secret recipe for the ridding of worms; it was an infusion in limewater of the powdered root of this fern, which is a treatment still in use today. Obviously a herb that shifts tapeworms has powerful compounds. These include thiaminase. It interferes with the production of thiamine (vitamin $B_1$), which is needed for the metabolism of carbohydrate. That does not show up when man takes a dose for worms but the more sustained use for treating children with rickets would not be recommended today. Similarly, in recent years, it has been dropped as an official flavouring agent. A deficiency of thiamine affects the brain and nervous system plus the heart and vascular system, and is best known as the forms of beriberi diseases. Problems will also arise when the body actually needs more than its usual level of thiamine, either due to other illnesses, such as liver disease, or simply during pregnancy and lactation. Severe cases lead to blindness and death. That is a concern where livestock can enter woodland, as was commonly the case with the old system of 'wood pasture' and is still the case with feral animals of the New Forest, but even livestock in fields can be risk if the field is hedged with the fern in the hedge-bottoms. It thrives in a wide range of habitats. Similar symptoms can occur after the ingestion of Bracken and so there's a danger of misidentifying the cause. However, Bracken dies down in the winter and leaves no crowns.

**Bracken** (*Pteridium aquilinum* L.) is one of our best-known poisonous plants and has also been described as our worst weed, invading hill pastures and taking a million acres a year out of use. Formerly it was a plant of the highest value. The rising crosiers in May were gathered by women and children as pig food while in July the women burnt the fronds to yield precious potash (potassium carbonate) for soaps, detergents, glass-making etc. and both these long-established activities lasted well into the 20th century, as did taking the litter in autumn for animal and human bedding. Thatchers took a harvest in September but such roofing seems to have died out in the 19th century as did making bread flour from the rhizomes, grubbed up during periods of adversity. Apparently such bread was very sustaining. With all these uses for Bracken it must have been at a premium in many places; indeed as late as the 1940s at least one set of villagers (in Surrey) came to blows over their allocation. With all this experience it is odd that the toxicity was not caused centuries of alarm over the fern but such has not been the case. Perhaps this is an instance where the continued depredations upon the plant stimulated higher levels of chemical defences. Perhaps areas of sweeter-tasting less-toxic Bracken were eaten to death and we are now left with the genetic strain that is more toxic. Certainly Bracken should not be eaten. Ignore the recipes published during the First World War since it was not known then that the fern would cause gastric cancers. The Japanese wondered why they had the highest incidence of gastric cancers in the world and this was traced back (with laboratory verification) to their enthusiasm for the spring-time crosiers as a delicacy. They consumed so much that they had to start importing it. The Japanese in London reportedly resorted to Richmond Park to gather theirs. In Canada and the United States it has been considered a delicacy too, calling the crosiers 'fiddleheads'. So although this book does not detail carcinogenic plants the Bracken has got to be an exception. Apart from cancers, humans consuming it can develop a haemorrhaging syndrome, the proportion of platelets in the blood falls, and the white blood cells develop a sort of anaemia, with a fall in bone marrow activity.

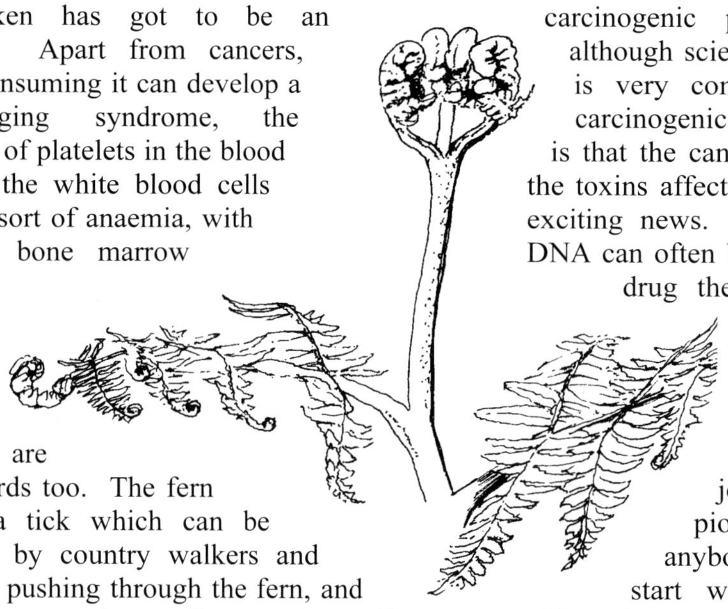

There are other hazards too. The fern harbours a tick which can be picked up by country walkers and their dogs, pushing through the fern, and this tick causes lyme disease, (council offices and libraries may have a leaflet about the dangers of lyme disease). It has long been known that grazing animals suffer from the Bracken because it contains thiaminase (see Male Fern). It does not affect ruminants (cattle) but it does affect horses and pigs, and so is a concern in places like the New Forest where pigs and ponies are feral. Another concern has been whether inhaling the fern spores will cause lung cancer. As far as could be traced, no direct link between the two has been established. It is a theoretical risk, knowing the make-up of compounds in the spores, but anyone anxious about this should desist from walking through Bracken for the three weeks or so of high summer when the spores are released, especially in years of mass sporing which occur about every three or four years. Outdoor workers among Bracken would be particularly at risk of course. We cannot avoid spores – they are everywhere, drifting around in the air currents, in our cities, up on the edge of the atmosphere, out over Antarctica. Animals can also pass on carcinogenic compounds from Bracken through their milk. It is not all doom and gloom though. We have known about the carcinogenic properties since 1960 and although scientific findings vary (the plant is very complex, having at least five carcinogenic compounds) the general view is that the cancer-causing activity is due to the toxins affecting the DNA. That could be exciting news. Molecules that damage the DNA can often be exploited as an anti-cancer drug themselves, by using them to destroy the DNA of the cancer cells. The same principles could also be of value in producing anti-viral drugs. It's a long journey of discovery though, pioneered by the Japanese and anybody wanting more detail could start with the work of Kiyoyuki Yamada, Iwao Hirono, Makoto Ojika, Haruki Niwa and Hideo Kigoshi.

The main compound that is interesting scientists in particular is known as ptaquiloside – a norsequiterpene glucoside. It can be persistent, poisoning the ground beneath the Bracken cover – nothing likes growing up through the litter – and it is now known that this can leach into the ground water and end up in wells and water courses. That said, the risk of contamination of British water is too small and too dilute to be a major cause of cancer, says Cancer Research UK. Water is tested vigorously and continuously by the Drinking Water Inspectorate. Similarly, milk is monitored stringently, knowing that some of the carcinogens can be passed on by cows through their milk. Work done on Bracken compost by Dr Rona Pitman for the Forestry Commission found that, if composted properly over the winter, the undesirable compounds degrade in the heat of the heap and the compost is safe to use next spring. Other research may lead to anti-fungal and insecticidal products that would be useful to the growers of 'organic' produce. Bracken is one of the World's commonest plants, found on every continent except Antarctica, and we have survived living with it so far. It can be dangerous and it does degrade agricultural and amenity land but it could prove to be a wonderful source of anti-cancer and anti-viral drugs and thereby cause celebration.

**Elder** (*Sambucus nigra* L.) yields the second most widespread folk harvest surviving today (after blackberries), with flowers and berries of importance for thousands of years. Archaeologists have found the residue of elderberries in Bronze Age pots, where it may it indicate usage for nutrition but may have been important in drink since the berries are the richest source in Britain of wild yeasts. Today the tree is enjoying a revival with new orchards being planted to provide flowers for cordials, berries for wine, etc. although economic demand still requires additional gathering of many tonnes each year from the wild. It is the berries that carry the hazard. The pips and green berries contain cyanogenic glycosides, such as sambunigrin, which release hydrocyanic acid under enzyme action. In other words, they can give you a dose of cyanide. Our forefathers knew there was a hazard and used the elderberries for wine and jelly only, since those products had the pips strained out of them. Modern writers, scorning this intelligence, have recommended strewing elderberries into apple pies. Probably that would not entail enough to cause harm but you won't know till you are unwell. Modern recipes for elderberry jam are far more worrying because there would be so many pips. There are reports on the Internet of poisonings after drinking the juice, where the berries have been crushed and thereby releasing the prussic acid. Always pick out the green berries and remove the pips and then you have a tasty and nutritious product that is also of medicinal value. That value has been recognised for thousands of years but came to the fore in 1631 with the publication in Latin of *Anatomia sambuci: or, The anatomie of the elder* by Dr Martin Blochwich. He gathered together what was known of the tree, over a range of disciplines from medicine to mythology. Then in 1655 he published a version in English, '*for the advancement of our language and medicines*.' It ran to a second edition in 1670, under recommendation of the Royal Society, *'for the benefit of all'*, and then a third edition in 1677. He includes knowledge of what we would now describe as stimulation of the immune system and it was this that modern science re-investigated in the quest for virus controls. The work was pioneered in Israel by the virologist Dr. Madeleine Mumcuoglu, who isolated and identified the active constituent. She went on to patent a procedure for its correct standardization and had it put through the necessary laboratory and clinical tests. It is marketed as SAMBUCOL™

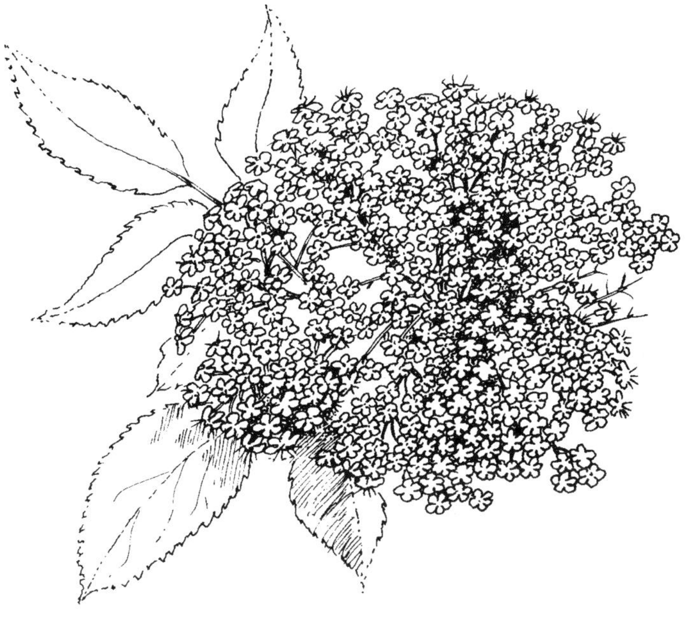

**Hawthorn**
*Crataegus monogyna* Jacq.
*Crataegus laevigata* (Poirot) DC.

The **Hawthorn** produces the beautiful white 'May Blossom' that has accrued so much folklore. From which we are to believe this is an 'unlucky' tree. Its inclusion in this book is open to question, since the Hawthorns are usually deemed to be so low in toxins as to be safe. However, these common trees have been included as a warning to those people who pick the young shoots in spring for garnishing their salads as 'bread and cheese'. They provide vitamin C and have a taste of bitter almonds, which should warn us not to eat a lot. This salad option is very well known but does not seem to be put into practice very often, which might be a good thing for anybody taking heart medicines. The trees contain compounds that affect the heart and are exploited for valuable cardiac medicines. Presumably taking extra doses, as a Hawthorn garnish, or in a preserve or wine made from the fruits should be avoided in case the action is contrary to a patient's prescribed drugs, especially digitoxin and digoxin. Hawthorn medicines are used to treat the early stages of congestive heart failure and angina, or during the recovery period after a heart attack. They are rated highly because they are have a more gentle action and are less toxic than some alternatives. Not only do they act directly on the heart muscle but they also dilate the blood vessels which can help reduce high blood pressure, especially by removing excess fluid through being diuretic. Thus they may also be employed during the treatment of kidney problems. Too much Hawthorn causes stomach upsets as a warning but normally it takes very large amounts to produce symptoms of poisoning.

**Foxgloves** (*Digitalis purpurea* L.)

As you read these words there must be several million people in the world who are only alive at the moment thanks to this powerful plant. It yields a range of closely related compounds that have a powerful and direct action upon our bodies, especially upon the heart and circulatory system. Now it's realised that people taking these drugs rarely develop cancer and so a whole new range of studies are in progress to ascertain the value of these compounds in oncology, especially breast cancer. The drugs developed from foxgloves rate in the top ten in the western world.

It is one of our most beautiful wild flowers too but perhaps we miss much of that beauty simply because of familiarity. It was an unknown flower to the American naturalist John Burroughs and so perhaps his description can open our eyes again: -

*"In travelling south from Scotland, the foxglove traveled [siq] as fast as I did, and I found it just as abundant in the southern counties as in the northern. This is the most beautiful and conspicuous of all the wild flowers I saw, a spire of large purple bells rising above the ferns and copses and along the hedges everywhere. Among the copses of Surrey and Hants, I saw it five feet high, and amid the rocks of Wales still higher. We have no conspicuous wild flower that compares with it. It is so showy and abundant that the traveler [siq] on the express train cannot miss it; while the pedestrian finds it lines his way like rows of torches..."*

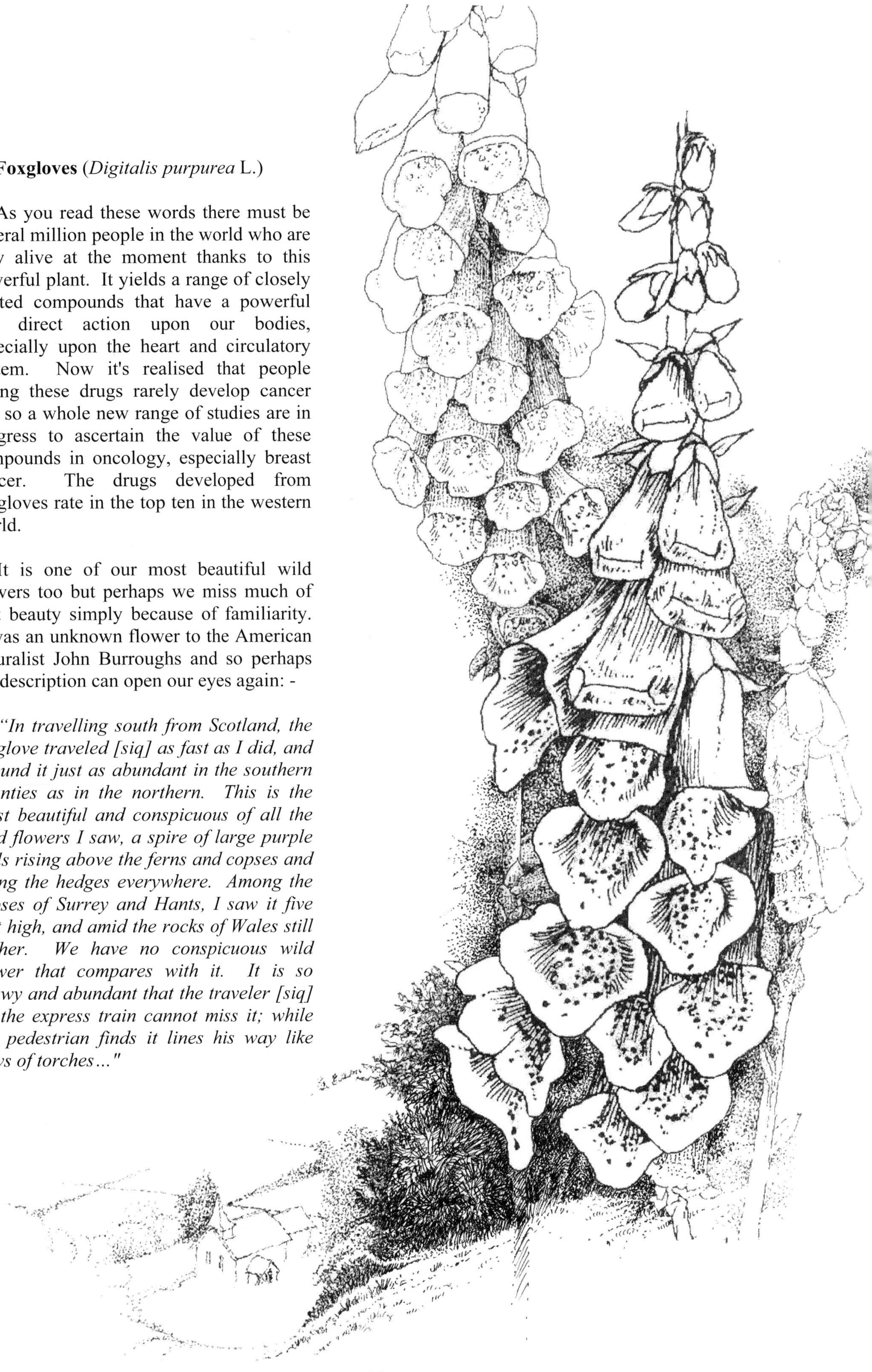

Foxgloves were introduced into the United States only after their medicinal value was realised, in the early 19th century. This is very much a wonder plant of modern times. The Greeks and Romans, who founded so much of our medicinal knowledge, do not seem to have used it. There doesn't even seem to be a name for it in classical writings. Here, the Saxons called it *foxes glofa* and *foxesclife* but used it little. Similarly the 13th century Welsh physicians at Myddfai used it only externally for scrofula. By the 18th century it was used in Shropshire folk medicine for dropsy and it was that treatment that caught the attention of Dr. William Withering.

William Withering (1741-1799) was not just a physician but also a leading botanist. He began his botanical studies in 1768 and in 1776 published his first book, *A Botanical Arrangement of all the Vegetables Naturally Growing in Great Britain with Descriptions of the Genera and Species according to Linnaeus*. This was the first complete British flora in English, as opposed to Latin, used by Johnson and Ray. Thus he was well-versed in British plants which led to him isolating Foxgloves in a remedy:-

*In the year 1775 my opinion was asked concerning a family recipe concerning the cure of dropsy. I was told that it had long been kept a secret by an old woman in Shropshire who had sometimes made cures after the more regular practitioners had failed. I was informed also that the effects produced violent vomiting and purging; for the diuretic effects seemed to have been overlooked. This medicine was composed of twenty or more different herbs; but it was not very difficult for one conversant in these subjects to perceive that the active herb could be no other than foxglove.*

Although Withering was the first to discover the value of foxgloves, he was not the first into print on the subject. That fell to Erasmus Darwin, grandfather of Charles Darwin, who gave no credit to Withering for the discovery, although "the evidence is undisputable". Not unexpectedly their relationship became acrimonious.

So for over two hundred years we've been exploring the Foxglove to discover the range of active compounds therein, so that now the original compound, called digitalin, is seen as part of a wider range. The most important is a highly active glycoside called digitoxin. It is used to strengthen the pumping action of weakening hearts. It achieves this by increasing the amount of calcium taken into the cells of the heart muscle. That makes it pump more strongly and more effectively. At the same time digitoxin makes sure the heart doesn't go into overdrive. It reduces the number of electrical impulses from the brain, driving the heart, and thereby slows it down. To this range we have been adding compounds from other Foxglove species, especially *Digitalis lanata*, with their varying reactions, to which we've added confusion by using different names for the same compound. Although the drugs can be synthesised for commercial production they have been found less effective than the drugs taken from the leaves and seeds of the plant. Therefore the pharmaceutical companies have fields of Foxgloves grown for them in N. W. Europe - but not in Britain.

*The foxglove's leaves, with caution given,*
*Another-proof: of favouring Heav'n*
*Will happily display,*
*The rapid pulse it can abate*
*The hectic flush can moderate*
*And blest by Him whose Will is fate*
*May give a lengthen'd day.*

(William Withering)

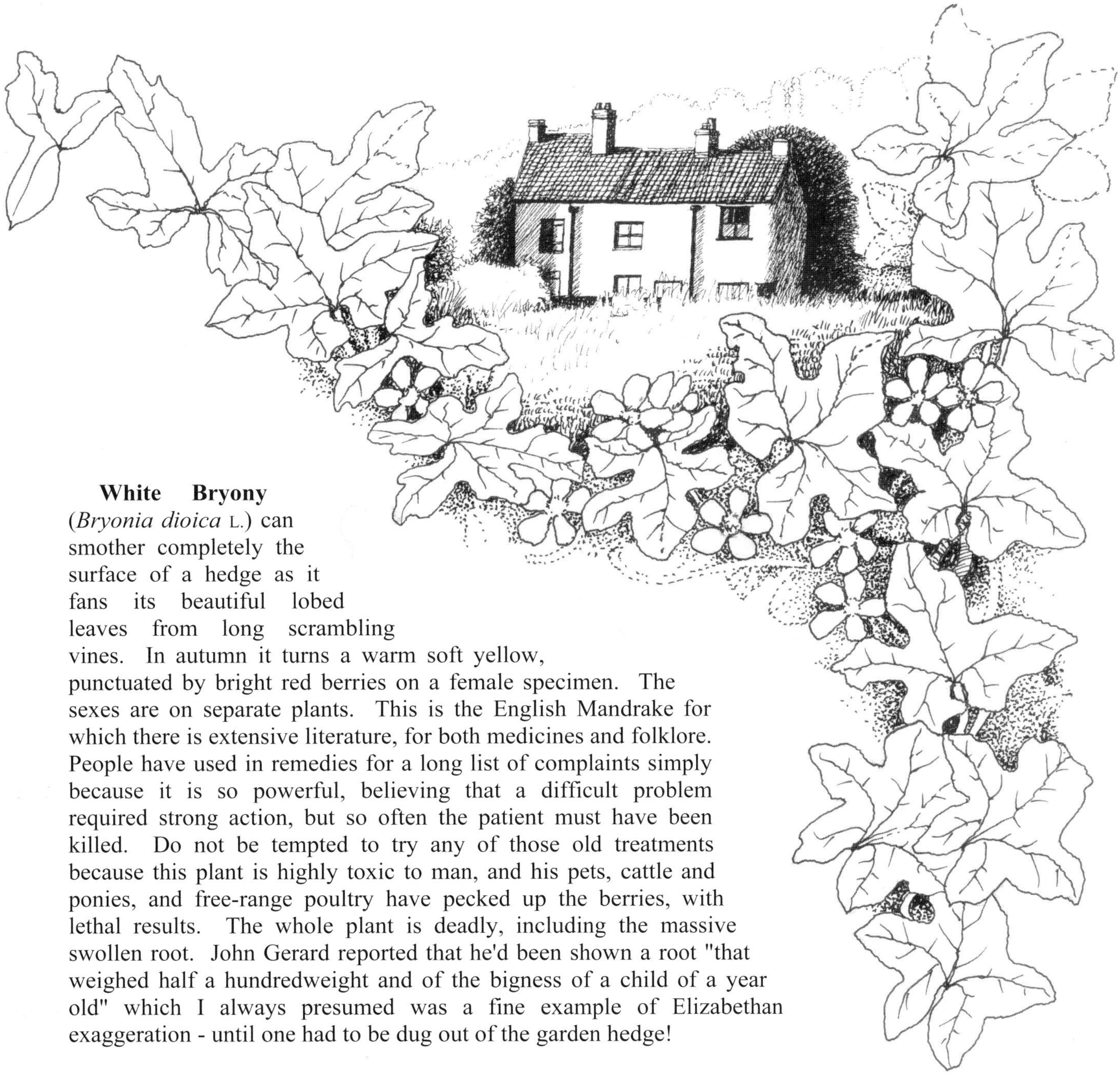

**White Bryony** (*Bryonia dioica* L.) can smother completely the surface of a hedge as it fans its beautiful lobed leaves from long scrambling vines. In autumn it turns a warm soft yellow, punctuated by bright red berries on a female specimen. The sexes are on separate plants. This is the English Mandrake for which there is extensive literature, for both medicines and folklore. People have used in remedies for a long list of complaints simply because it is so powerful, believing that a difficult problem required strong action, but so often the patient must have been killed. Do not be tempted to try any of those old treatments because this plant is highly toxic to man, and his pets, cattle and ponies, and free-range poultry have pecked up the berries, with lethal results. The whole plant is deadly, including the massive swollen root. John Gerard reported that he'd been shown a root "that weighed half a hundredweight and of the bigness of a child of a year old" which I always presumed was a fine example of Elizabethan exaggeration - until one had to be dug out of the garden hedge!

The toxins are complex but include glycosides, known as bryonodin, bryonin, bryonicine etc. These are strongly irritant and cause vomiting if children eat the berries. This is another plant they should be taught to leave well alone. The disturbing list of symptoms culminates in death through respiratory failure. It's not all grim though. The plant has been investigated to see if it would yield compounds that inhibit cancer tumours, once the effective compounds have been separated from the toxins. Otherwise the plant is avoided nowadays since it is not known how much is a 'safe' dose, and there is no antidote. Some trained herbalists use it sparingly today but homoeopaths use a different species altogether. Only goats are said to eat this plant with immunity which is scarcely credible. More believable is Augustus Caesar wearing a wreath of it to protect himself from lightning!

**Old Man's Beard** (*Clematis vitalba* L.) can hummock over hedge tops and cascade out of trees on the sunny side of woodlands. The flowers have none of the glamour of the garden cultivars but the Wild Clematis becomes conspicuous in the winter, when the low sun shines through the whitish fluffy seedheads. It starts off in shrubby places where it can climb up over a host, keeping its head in the sun but its feet in the shade. If the host grows up to be a tree then it takes the clematis up with it, to 30 metres, so that shaggy-barked 'liana vines' add verticals through the woodland scene. All parts of the plant are toxic but it's the greenery that poses the risk for it can be lethal to livestock browsing the hedge. Fortunately, they don't often eat much of it because it tastes bitter and burns the mouth, due to protoanemonine, since this too belongs to the buttercup family. It has been used in herbal medicines and there are reports of people using it still. However, there are better herbal treatments available that do not put the patient at so much risk.

**Black Bryony** (*Tamus communis* L.). Although a perennial it does die down each winter and send up long (up to 4m) stems each year. They barely get noticed, until its dark glossy green leaves turn bright butter yellow and some will even be purple. The clusters of berries ripen from green into brilliant red but be wary of this beauty. The whole plant is toxic. Least of all are the young shoots in the spring, which have been eaten as a substitute for Asparagus but they are best avoided. It is not known for certain which toxins it contains. It used to be thought that these were saponins but more recent texts doubt that the saponins are responsible and now the toxicity is presumed to derive from glycosides. The plant springs each year from a massive black tuber (up to 60cm) which reminds us this plant is the only British 'Yam' but do not eat this tuber. It's extremely bitter and too much results in a very painful death. It's been tried as a medicine, being a powerful diuretic, but this plant is really too violent to use. The level of toxicity can vary and so can the responses of different patients, so it's impossible to determine a safe dose. The plant contains hystamine or a histamine-like compound, which is implicated in allergic reactions. Too much of that dilates the capillaries, lowers blood pressure and affects breathing, to hasten the other toxic effects. Some of those effects come from oxalic acid, which can be absorbed through the skin so do not handle the greenery too much. In the blood, it combines with calcium to produce

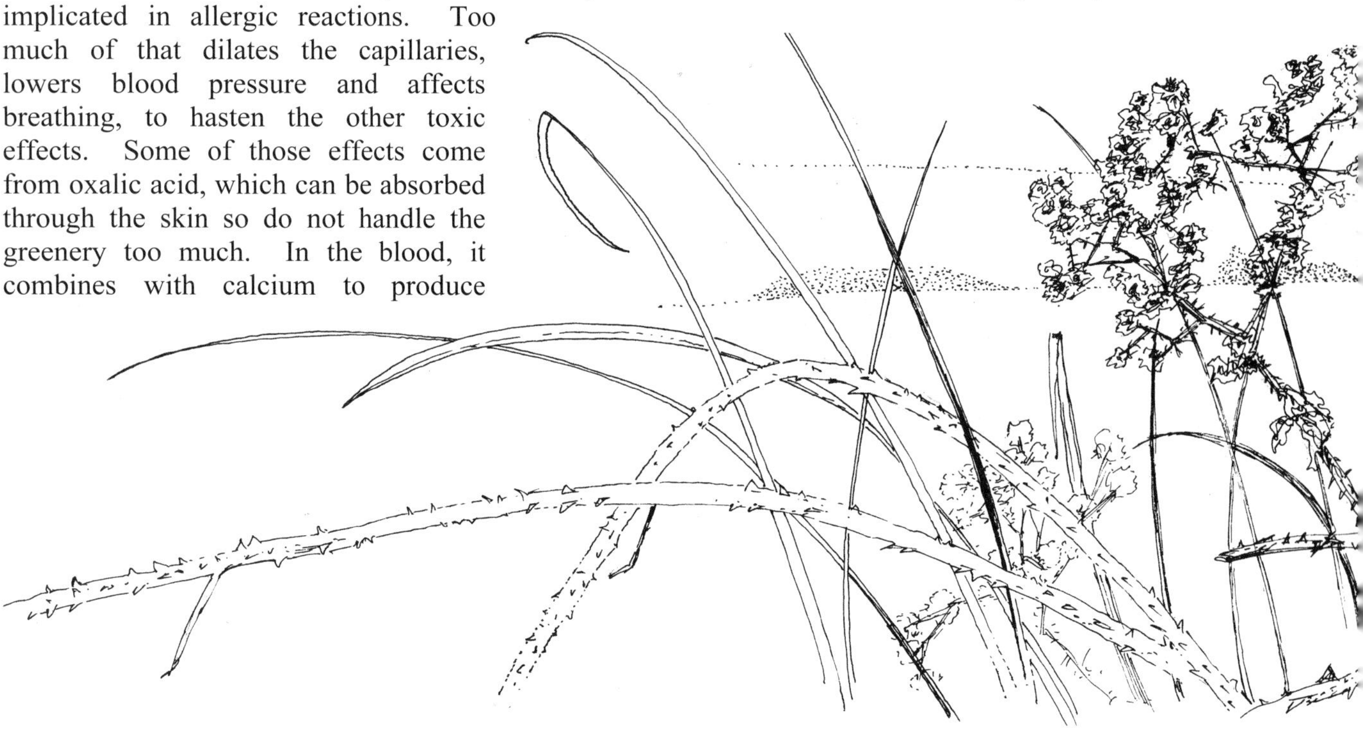

calcium oxalate crystals, which clog up your kidneys. It is the berries that are most likely to be eaten and in these the calcium oxalate crystals are more concentrated, so teach children not to eat them. They burn the mouth and cause swelling which can block the airway. However, the plant is strongly purgative and so the child is likely to be saved by vomiting. Horses and cattle have been less fortunate and fatalities are recorded, so hedges around paddocks and pastures should be checked for the distinctive glossy, pointed, heart-shaped leaves.

**Blackberries** (*Rubus fruticosus* aggr.) are still the most popular wild harvest and are perfectly safe to eat, until the end of September. Then the onset of autumn, with shorter days, cooler, moister nights, promotes the growth of fungi. Just as the toadstools pop up in the woodlands so the moulds, yeasts and other fungal growths proliferate over the sugary Blackberry fruits. At this stage they can cause stomach upsets and allergic reactions in some people. That was well known to our ancestors, who blamed it on Satan, saying never to pick blackberries after Michaelmas Eve (28th September) because the Devil will have peed on them. The exact wording of the lore varies from district to district and sometimes the date, as in Surrey where 25th September marks the end of the season. This should have been known to the countryman George Sturt yet in his journal he records walking out of Farnham to Puttenham Common on 29th (1891) and gathering blackberries. He probably ate them the next day because he records, "*Sick in the night; and 'queer' all yesterday morning: not well, indeed, all day.*"

# GRASSY SUNNY PLACES

Open places are frequently dominated by grasses, nurturing among them a great diversity of more colourful wild flowers. When the wind strokes swathes of them into gentle waves through the sunlight the day seems perfect for a moment or two. All it needs are the village people hurrying out to mow, as in all those old paintings and early photographs that have created a mythic Golden Age of times past. In truth, all hands worked hard to beat the rain clouds. Hay was the only winter feed for the livestock until the 17th century and so the well-being of each community depended upon it. Fathers taught their sons how to sharpen and use a scythe as soon as they were big enough to handle one and as the crop fell so everybody kept a sharp watch for any of the notorious poisonous plants. Some of these are rendered safe by drying while others have their toxicity concentrated. Today we are more familiar with fodder grass and silage, which are the most efficient means of producing protein in Britain, since grass grows through all but the coldest weather and doesn't need ripening in sunshine, like cereals. The cereals are all grasses, so this family of plants is the most important in the world. It is fortunate that out of the 150 or so grasses in Britain only one, Darnel, has been thought poisonous and that is not a pasture grass but a weed of disturbed places.

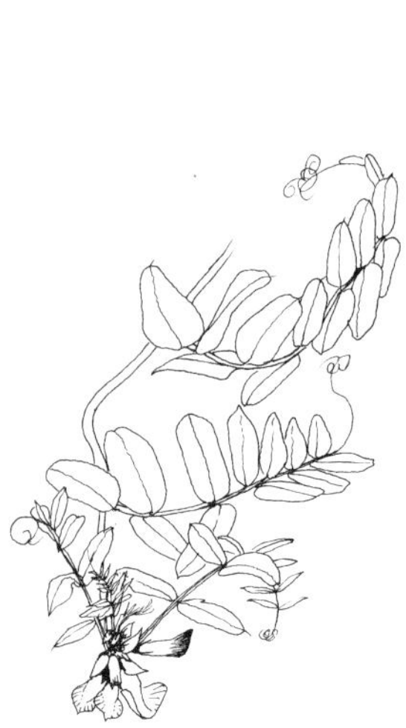

That does not mean grass is entirely safe. Even if the species do not contain toxins as such, they can be deleterious to health, especially lush spring grass or an autumn flush. This can cause 'bloat' in ruminants and be fatal. Horses are not susceptible but are at risk from laminitis (and sometimes colic) caused by the concentrated fructins. To render lush grass safe the fructins needs to go through a proper fermentation process - silage for ruminants and haylage for horses. Another set of hazards arise from the micro-species of fungi associating with them, and more particularly those found in mouldy hay. Traditionally it was always deemed unwise to feed mouldy hay and modern science is proving that right as the species involved are being identified and matched with poor health conditions in livestock. This work is nowhere near complete. To highlight one example, the **Sweet Vernal Grass** (*Anthoxanthum odoratum* L) is a very common and important

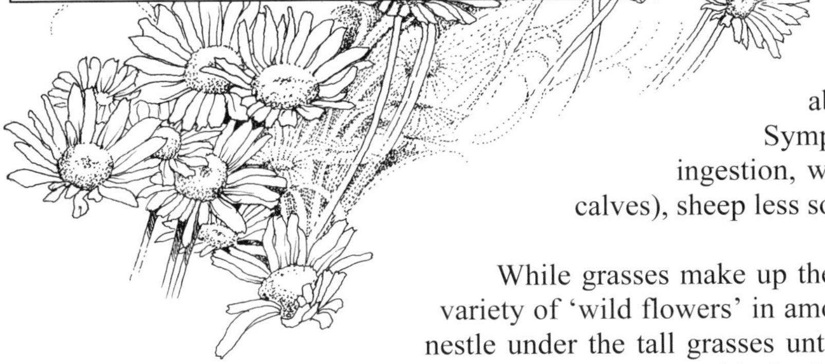

species in British grasslands, producing plenty of good forage early in the year. It contains compounds not met with so far in this book, the coumarins. These are aromatic and give the characteristic smell to both new-cut grass and to hay. They make the hay appetising and so encourage livestock to feed when they might otherwise be bored silly with it. Should it be mouldy though, the fungi (particularly species of *Penicillium*, *Mucor* and *Aspergillus*) can convert the coumarins into dicoumarol and that is seriously toxic. It inhibits the action of vitamin K, which is vital in the chain reaction of blood-clotting, allowing both internal and external haemorrhaging. Obviously that can be lethal. It can also cause abortions and can cross the placenta. Symptoms start to show 24-36 hours after ingestion, with cattle most susceptible (especially calves), sheep less so and horses rarely.

While grasses make up the bulk of the hay, there is also a wide variety of 'wild flowers' in among them. Some are much shorter and nestle under the tall grasses until they are cut. Then they flourish as 'bottom growth', to provide fresh forage much quicker than it takes the grasses to produce quantities of leaf blades again. Good bottom growth was a boon in the past since it meant livestock could be returned to the meadows faster since wherever they had been in the meantime required space and feed, both of which could be at a premium. The idea gets developed as one of the 'Improvements' of the 17th century. It centred on those plants which had nodules of bacteria on their roots (the legumes) which take nitrogen gas out of the air and convert it into solid nitrogen compounds that enrich the soil to maintain fertility. That feeds the harvested crop back into quick growth but can make the plant high in nitrates. That can be a problem since ruminants digest the nitrates into nitrites and these combine in the blood with the oxygen-carrying haemoglobin. The new compound is called methaemaglobin and can be lethal since it does not carry oxygen. The vast majority of the legumes belong to the pea and bean family, classified in older texts as the Leguminoseae and in more recent texts as the Fabaceae, named after *Faba*, the bean. Apart from beans (of the Broad Bean type) the family includes the trefoils, clovers and vetches and it was these that became

important in British agriculture. One of the chief pioneers was Sir Richard Weston of Sutton Place, Guildford, Surrey. Unfortunately he was both a Catholic and a Royalist when the Puritan Parliament was in power. So when he was not in exile he had to keep a rather low profile, working away on his land improvements and also producing a written account. This he had published anonymously in 1645 by Samuel Hartlib under the title, *Directions for the Improvement of Barren Land.* However in 1651 Hartlib re-issued the book under the title, *Enlargement of the Discourse of Husbandry used in Brabant and Flanders - Sir Richard Weston's Legacy to his Sons.* The next year Weston died and Hartlib issued a third printing, changing the title politically to *A Discourse of Husbandry used in Brabant and Flanders: showing the wonderful improvements of land there; and serving as a pattern for our practice in this commonwealth.* It recorded Weston's assessment of his pioneering work in agriculture on his estates at Sutton Place. Here is the first mention of growing clover deliberately to increase and enrich the yield of the land. As the title suggests, this was already practised across the North Sea and it was to these Low Countries that Sir Richard had travelled to use up his youthful energies. Obviously he noted how the Dutch were earning a better return off their land than was his father back home. Shortly after Richard's return his father died and upon inheriting the lands Richard could begin a programme of 'improvements'.

He worked principally with **Red Clover** (*Trifolium* pratense L) which he calls Great Clovers (*illus. above*), implying there was a lesser one. Indeed he does record using one and although he offers no description it is believed to be the **White Clover** (*Trifolium repens* L.) (*illus.round hedgehog!*). This is also known as Dutch Clover, which may derive from its introduction into agriculture from practices in the Low Countries. When colonists from Britain took our practices round the world problems arose over the White Clover and it seemed to be toxic. Certainly there are species which are toxic in one country and not in another. Investigations into this plant have now determined that the plant is polymorphic – having one type that is cyanogenic and one that is not. The cyanogenic glucosides are laminarin and lotaustralin which get hydrolysed by the enzyme linamarase to produce the deadly hydrogen cyanide. The presence of the glucosides is determined by genetics, as is the inheritance of the enzyme. Even plants that inherit both the dominant genes are found to be variable which again is due in part to the genetics but also to environmental factors such as light intensity, moisture, temperature and phosphorus. Fortunately the risk of grazing animals suffering direct cyanide poisoning has found to be low but the cyanide metabolites can interfere with selenium and iodine levels, and have been implicated in a muscle-wasting condition. In addition White Clover contains small amounts of coumestrol which can either interfere with reproduction or be a growth stimulant but levels are believed to be too low to cause concern. Looking on the bright side, the cyanogenic action wards off invertebrates and therefore reduces the need for farmers to use insecticides. Nevertheless the use of White Clover declined in Britain until the 1960s, due partly to the successful promotion of chemical fertilizers, but by then prices of inorganic nitrogen were rising sharply and there was an increasing awareness that chemicals were not actually the solution to all the farmer's problems. As the *Farmers Weekly* (5.4.1985) said, there was a "better understanding of the relationship between the sward quality and animal production" as it reported "the marketing move" of the National Seed Development Organisation and four commercial seed houses. It was to launch *Ensign*: a seed mixture of four prime varieties of white clover ('Menna', 'Nesta', 'Olwen' and 'Donna') which had been on the recommended list of the National Institute of Agricultural Botany since the late 1970s. They were bred on for 'Ensign' by Dr Ian Rhodes at the Welsh Plant Breeding Station at Aberystwyth. Today it is still an important plant.

Before turning to the Trefoils, a pause to note that Sir Richard Weston was a Roman Catholic recusant, in what was a new Protestant era. He was not singular in that but no doubt he and other estate owners still had lingering beliefs from their Catholic upbringings. These gave them a predisposition to favour the deliberate growing of Clovers and Trefoils because the trifoliate leaves had traditionally been viewed as a reminder from God of the Holy Trinity. Add a fourth leaflet, to make the shape of the Cross and that seen as something particularly auspicious. To find a four-leaved clover in the field was taken as a sign of God’s protection. People took such leaves as a ‘buttonhole’ to ward off evil and protect from witchcraft. Even today people look out for a ‘four-leafed clover’ and deem it a ‘lucky’ find. In the 17th century they could see (even if they didn’t have the science to understand fully) that these plants helped their husbandry prosper and that was taken as confirmation of God’s blessing.

**Bird's-foot Trefoil** (*Lotus corniculatus* L.) is a little beauty on sunny banks and pastures where it doesn't get smothered out by taller vegetation. It was brought into agricultural usage to mix with grass seed when sowing new pastures and was also grown deliberately as a forage crop under the corn. Other closely-related species were included, such as the **Narrow-leaved Trefoil**, (*Lotus glabra* Miller) and the **Greater Bird's-foot Trefoil** (*Lotus pendunculatus* Cav.). Beware the species in the genus *Lotus* have been through name changes so check carefully if this group is important to you. There are cultivar names in agricultural use too, such as 'Norcen', because this is still a plant viewed as having agricultural merit and work continues today to develop good strains. Some of these are identified by numbers rather than names. Again, the whole plant contains cyanogenic glycosides, and these have been investigated around the world with varying results from country to country. In general most research confirms that the highest concentrations are found in the flowers and the leaves while the seed pods, strangely enough, having the least. Concentrations are highest in spring and lessen as summer proceeds. It was, therefore, safer in the days when it was grazed after hay-making. Similarly, when they began sowing members of this family with the corn, to provide forage immediately after the harvest, it was again late in the year when the plant was safest. Although we read that the animals were turned onto the stubble to "eat the weeds" they were not just 'weeds' and there was far more science involved that we usually credit. The livestock do not seem to realise the plant can be noxious because it's not until digestion is underway that problems arise. As the vegetation is broken down so compounds are able to mix and hydrolise, causing the cyanogenic glycosides to produce hydrocyanic acid. In small amounts this improves digestion but too much results in respiratory failure and death.

Brilliant golden Buttercup meadows are another one of those scenes that people take to their hearts. The first flush of the season, in bright gold, comes from the **Bulbous Buttercup** (*Ranununculus bulbosus* L) and the **Creeping Buttercup** (*Ranunculus repens L*) followed by a second, taller flush, in a softer gold of **Meadow Buttercups** (*Ranunculus acris* L). Such massed flowerings only occur because the plants are poisonous. They taste acrid and so the livestock avoid eating them, thus allowing them to come up to flower. Should the animals start to run out of other fodder then they have to start on the Buttercups and soon get a liking for their bitter taste. Members of this family produce the glycoside ranunculin, which is very toxic to mammals. Damaging the foliage, by chewing it, releases enzymes that change the ranunculin into a highly irritant volatile oil, called protoanemonine. This compound is unstable and changes again, into anemonine, and that is non-toxic. By then though, the caustic stage may already have caused severe irritation and blistering. It's rendered harmless by drying and so it is not a problem in hay. That said, the reports of poisoning in livestock are far fewer than we might expect and scientific studies produce widely varying results. In one experiment feeding buttercups to cattle actually increased their weight, with no ill effects. Consequently farmers are not usually worried about the Buttercups but the grazing ought to be watched to ensure there are sufficient alternatives to feed upon. There is one odd bit of folklore that says rubbing buttercups into a cow's udder will produce more milk. Surely there would be a very different reaction if you rubbed a caustic herb into the soft udder! By way of explanation it has been suggested that it means dusting the udder with pollen from a bunch of flowers because the calf will find that bitter, wean more quickly, and leave more milk for the farmer. Another piece of history is recalled in the name St. Anthony's Turnip for the Bulbous Buttercup, alluding to the swollen stem-base. These 'bulbs' were gathered as food in famine years but the toxins burnt the mouth, reminding people of St. Anthony's fires of torment. Finally, if Buttercups have over-run a garden plot beware of weeding out large amounts by hand, especially if your skin is soft and sensitive.

Chickens scratching and pecking around a farmyard is another one of those emotive scenes from our collective folk memory. Some readers can look back nostalgically to hunting for the eggs or going to feed the hens in war-time chicken-runs. Poultry are less susceptible to our poisonous plants than other livestock because although they peck at greenery their main food is seed. Berries, such as Yew or from the Bryonies are a hazard when they scatter on the ground below, especially if it's inside a chicken run. Otherwise few plants provide enough toxic seeds in ways that threaten poultry but the potential of **Docks** should not be overlooked. They love the bare patches or rich soil around farmyards and even poultry in runs may find Docks have been allowed to grow up alongside. Each Dock plant can produce hundreds of seeds and they are large enough for poultry to feed upon, as they scatter on the ground around the plants. They are not well designed for wind-dispersal.

Docks contain oxalic acid and other oxalates which can lead to renal failure and so out in the grasslands they are a threat to the livestock. They taste bitter and astringent so they are not readily grazed but that just allows them to flourish better and suppress more desirable sward. Thus the **Broad-leaved Dock** (*Rumex obtusifolius* L) and the **Curled Dock** (*Rumex crispus* L) are specified in the 1959 Weeds Act but all members of the genus *Rumex* are rich in oxalates, so leave them alone. That said, there are historical references to people eating the leaves and grinding the tap roots for flour during famine years. Just because they ate them does not mean they survived. The effect is usually cumulative and so deaths would have been attributed to the famine in general. The Docks *are* nutritive, providing fibre and vitamins and a range of minerals drawn up by those great tap roots and so today they get promoted as a desirable 'wild food'. Indeed one web site veritably extols the Curled Dock. Do not be fooled by statements such as, "*No human toxicity has ever been reported*" because it *has* and even fatality. Docks have been, and still are, used widely around the world in herbal medicines. These applications are less worrying because only small amounts are used and in a controlled way, providing the patient is following professional guidance and not trying a do-it-yourself remedy.

**Ragwort**
(*Senecio jacobaea* L.) is the great emotive plant at the moment. Hatred for our poisonous plants goes in phases. Not so long ago there were massed fears over the Laburnum, then it was the Yew tree until it proved valuable against cancer and people warmed to it and now it is the Ragwort. When leading guided walks I hear people say "Oh is that what Ragwort looks like? That's deadly isn't it." No it's not, except to livestock, of which horses are particularly susceptible. I've seen people pull children away from the plant, saying "It's dangerous." Children are not at risk because it tastes absolutely foul and they would need to eat such a lot. So let us have a more rational look at the plant.

Ragwort becomes noticeable when it bolts up to flower, for it can reach one and a half metres, and has a more or less flat-topped corymb of brazen gold-yellow daisy flowers. They are an ideal nectar source for insects, which need no special adaptations to reach it. This makes Ragwort a very significant plant to the survival of British wildlife in all its diversity. English Nature has listed 117 species that feed upon this nectar, including butterflies and bees. Some species are dependent upon it and some are national rarities. One reason why it is so important is not just that it provides so much nectar, easily accessed, but because it blooms from high summer onwards, when so many other nectar sources have finished flowering. The leaves feed a list of 77 species and again these include dependants and rarities. An ecologist can sing prolonged praises for this plant. Horse-owners and livestock farmers do not. To them it is the most highly dangerous plant their animals may commonly encounter in this country.

The toxins are distributed throughout the plant and derive from pyrrolizidine alkaloids, (e.g. senecionine, seneciphylline, jacoline, jaconine, jacobine, and jacozine). The purpose of these alkaloids in the plant is not understood unless it is purely to safeguard it from being eaten, in which case it is not altogether successful, judging by the totals given above. These alkaloids are not poisonous in themselves but produce lethal metabolites when they are broken down in the body, at which time they can also produce toxic alcohols, as secondary metabolites. They cause liver failure but also affect the heart, kidneys and respiratory system. These effects are cumulative from repeated ingestion of the Ragwort so that symptoms may not show immediately and can be brief, making death appear sudden. However, a single large ingestion of Ragwort can also be lethal. Drying it in hay does not render it safe. It could even be worse because it is more palatable. Horses are most susceptible, followed by cattle and then sheep, with cases from other animals difficult to trace. Normally animals avoid the stinking, foul-tasting Ragwort and graze all around it to leave the golden-topped sentinels to

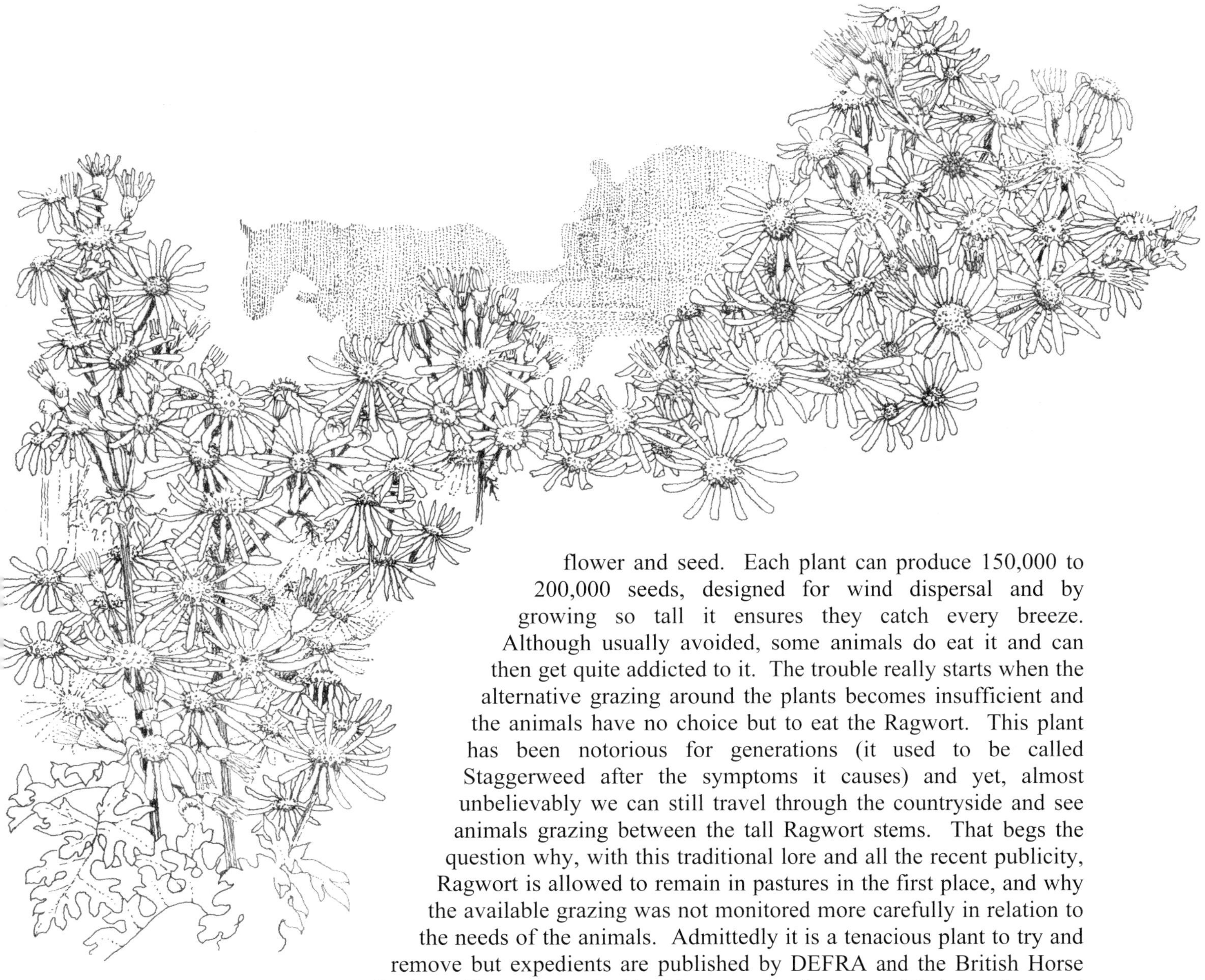

flower and seed. Each plant can produce 150,000 to 200,000 seeds, designed for wind dispersal and by growing so tall it ensures they catch every breeze. Although usually avoided, some animals do eat it and can then get quite addicted to it. The trouble really starts when the alternative grazing around the plants becomes insufficient and the animals have no choice but to eat the Ragwort. This plant has been notorious for generations (it used to be called Staggerweed after the symptoms it causes) and yet, almost unbelievably we can still travel through the countryside and see animals grazing between the tall Ragwort stems. That begs the question why, with this traditional lore and all the recent publicity, Ragwort is allowed to remain in pastures in the first place, and why the available grazing was not monitored more carefully in relation to the needs of the animals. Admittedly it is a tenacious plant to try and remove but expedients are published by DEFRA and the British Horse Society. Horses are valuable things, not just in terms of their purchase and upkeep, but in their emotional value when they are much-loved and of course people who work horses for a living have an added investment in them. Blaming the weed for deaths is no excuse for bad husbandry. As the British Horse Society says on its website, "*The horse owner has a very clear duty to protect his stock from what can only be described as a horrible and unnecessary death.*" Animals in our care need us to take care.

So how large a problem is this plant? That question became political and so there's a severe risk of distortion in the information being made public. Back in 1990 the Ministry figures recorded just ten horse fatalities whereas by 2005 the website for the British Horse Society was claiming "*Ragwort is thought to have caused the death of 500 horses in 2001, with the toll predicted at 1,000 for this year.*" Whether the Ministry is trying to minimise the risks and the British Horse Society has been inflating them in their efforts to get further legislation against the plant misses the point of the individual horse-owner's duty of care. The problem is not new. Back in 1959 Parliament passed the Weeds Act, which specifies five injurious weeds, namely Spear Thistle, Creeping or Field Thistle, Broad leaved Dock, Curled Dock and the Common Ragwort. The Act gave the Secretary of State powers to serve an enforcement notice on the occupier of land on which injurious weeds are growing, requiring the occupier to take action to prevent the spread of those weeds. Thus it is DEFRA that serves such clearance notices but normally only does so where agricultural production is affected directly. There is plenty of Ragwort territory that does not fall into this ambit, ranging from the Local Authority's roadside verges to National Trust land and Nature Reserves. Ragwort is spreading like wildfire – everybody says so! Is it true? Certainly I've seen masses of it where there was never any before but apparently this is a false impression: the overall view is that the Ragwort population has remained relatively stable. The Countryside Survey (funded by the Government) for the period 1990-1998 *"found no specific evidence of an increase in the frequency of Ragwort in fertile or infertile grassland."* They did find an increase *"in lowland woods and on arable land over that period, but these are both habitats where Ragwort abundance is comparatively low and which are not frequently grazed by horses The perceived increase in Ragwort abundance seems to be simply a result of increasing awareness resulting from the anti-Ragwort campaign."* Heightened public awareness may also be taking note that Ragwort will quickly colonise sites of temporary habitat status, such as redevelopment sites, set-aside land, and places where land usage is undergoing change. If the vegetation is sparse the Ragwort germinates readily without shade and competition and produces thick plantations of itself that are so very striking when in full bloom. These sites come and go quickly but leave the perception that Ragwort is on the rampage.

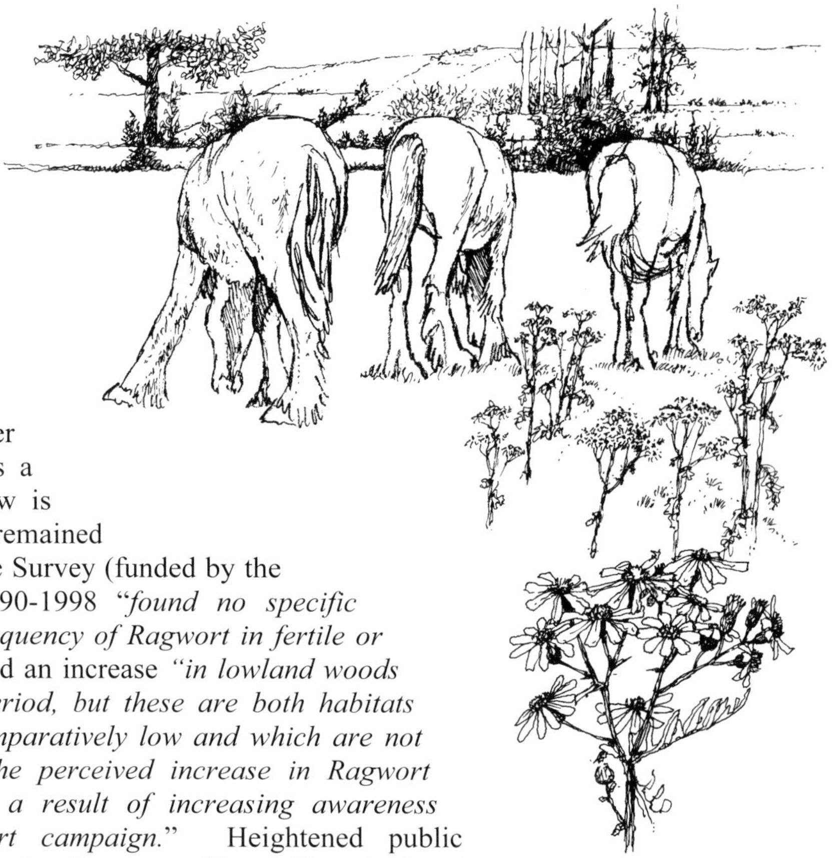

The British Horse Society initiated moves to tighten up the provision of the 1959 Weed Act by sponsoring a Private Members' Bill, (Ragwort Control Bill) which was taken through the House of Commons by John Greenway MP, and then through the House of Lords by Baroness Masham of Ilton. It gained Royal Assent on 20th November 2003 as the Ragwort Control Act and came into force in February 2004. It provides for a Code of Practice, and that has been formulated by the co-operative efforts of DEFRA and the British Horse Society. All this has been towards the *control* of Ragwort, not its eradication. It should not be rendered an endangered species since so many other species depend upon it. It is a very valuable plant to our wildlife and this has been detailed fully on the website of the Invertebrate Conservation Trust.

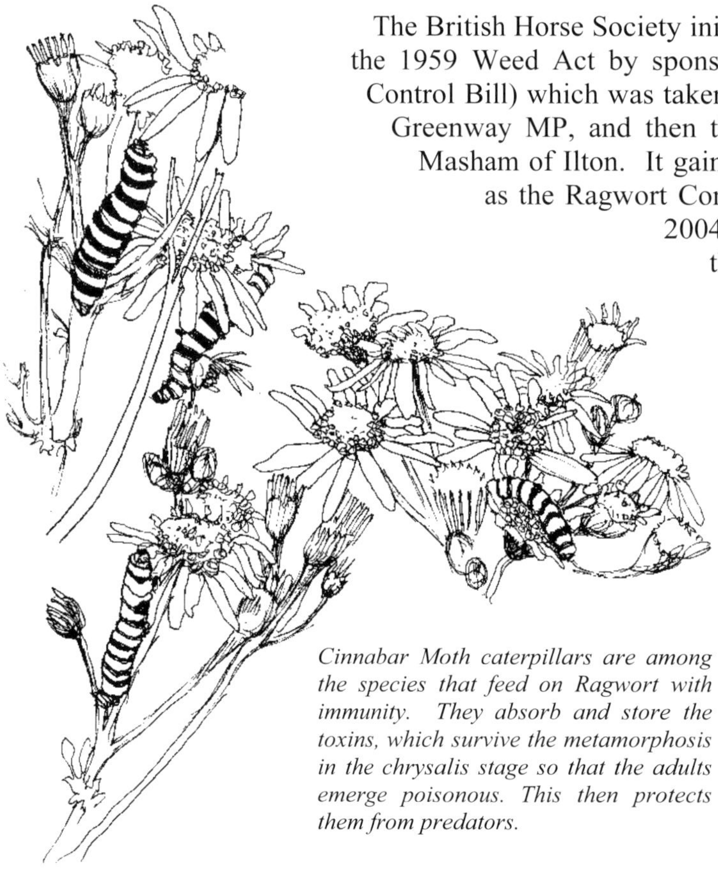

*Cinnabar Moth caterpillars are among the species that feed on Ragwort with immunity. They absorb and store the toxins, which survive the metamorphosis in the chrysalis stage so that the adults emerge poisonous. This then protects them from predators.*

The above notes apply also to the other species and hybrids of Ragwort in Britain. In the same genus is the humble little **Groundsel** which you'll find in the 'Disturbed Places' section.

**St. John's Wort** (*Hypericum perforatum* L.) has become one of the best-known medicinal herbs in Europe, in recent years, but is one that must be used with guidance and caution. Many people in Britain know it only from the warnings given out on the News a few years ago. Our ancestors knew it well as a 'powerful' plant. It was one of the most important 'protective' plants to ward off evil forces, indicated by its very name *Hypericum*, which comes from the ancient Greek meaning to overcome the image. It blooms in June and so was deemed essential for the Midsummer rituals, when spirit forces were believed to be very active and especially potent. It was not something that could be given up easily with the advent of Christianity and so the plant had to be Christianised. Along with some of the other Midsummer ritual plants it was dedicated to St. John the Baptist, whose Feast Day was 24th June. It is the only one of those plants to take on the saint's name which gives an indication of the prime importance given to it. Another reason was the association with blood, since the plants contain glands containing a translucent oil (the little 'perforations' in the leaves when they are held up to the light that give the plant its species name) which oxidizes blood red if the gland is broken and exposed to the air, just like the severed head of the executed saint.

To choose this plant in particular for ritual meaning was surely not at random for the plant contains compounds so powerful they affect the brain and its emotions. The chemistry of the plant is highly complex and provokes a bewildering sequence of reactions in our bodies when it is consumed. Most famously, it is anti-depressant but it is also anti-viral and anti-retroviral, and has anti-cancer activity too, and that's not the end of it. Traditionally it has been used in folk medicines for a long list of treatments down to antiseptic wound dressings. However, anything that affects the brain should be treated with caution and this is particularly so for St. John's Wort. Among its actions are several that inhibit normal functions in the brain. Specifically it affects the system by which brain messages are transmitted, which is performed by three monoamines, known individually as serotonin, norepinephrine, and dopamine Once these have completed their task they are destroyed by an enzyme from the liver and brain, called monoamine oxidase and St. John's Wort inhibits this destruction. Consequently, higher levels of these monoamines build up, which act as an anti-depressant since depression is associated with low levels of monoamines. Of course the concept of depression encompasses a broad field of problems and St. John's Wort is definitely not a cure-all for them. Even if it might be a suitable treatment caution must be exercised in relation to any other medication being taken at the same time since their actions are not compatible. It was that danger that hit the News headlines. This is because monoamine oxidase does not just destroy the three neurotransmitters listed above but affects another amine called tyramine, which affects blood pressure. If St John's Wort inhibits the monoamine oxidase so that allows levels of tyramine to

rise and so does the blood pressure, quite suddenly, until the vessels burst as brain haemorrhages etc. Now it becomes clearer why this herb should not be used in conjunction with medications controlling blood pressure etc., such as warfarin and some anti-convulsants but the herb has far reaching effects and so its anti-viral activities are not compatible with HIV treatments. It even affects oral contraceptives which might be overlooked in the 'other medications' category. There's a long list. The plant sounds ghastly but when used expertly it is certainly a wild flower to celebrate. Going back to the plant's content of hypericine which oxidises blood red, note that getting too much on your hands can make them sensitive to light (photosensitivity) resulting in sores that might become infected following rubbing or scratching. In severe cases the skin splits and the chunks between slough off. It is usually the unpigmented parts of the skin that react most. People who are prone to sunburn should take particular care. It affects grazing livestock too, especially those with a white coat, and is considered one of the most dangerous of the photosensitizing plants. Drying the fodder to hay reduces the toxicity by about 80% but even the remainder can be more than enough. That applies more to foreign countries, such as America (where it's known as Klamath Weed), since in Britain the plant does not often form extensive colonies but is patchy through the grassland. However, recent trends to leave field borders as strips of wildlife refuge might suit St. John's Wort and become a problem if livestock are returned to the field. Certainly in recent times it has taken to colonising rapidly the bare earth of new roundabouts getting it the name 'Roundabout Plant' from Sussex to Norfolk and beyond. Why it tends to shun the strips of dual carriageway linking the roundabouts has not been explained yet, but observation will soon reveal this is definitely a roundabout plant!

How few really poisonous plants there are amid the wealth of wild flowers and grasses of the open sunny places. It's a case of safety in numbers. The dominant plants are the grasses which belong to the monocotyledonous group, which grow from the base, so if the tops gets mown off, grazed or nibbled by caterpillars they just keep growing regardless. The broad-leaved plants, on the other hand, are dicotyledonous and grow from the tips. If these get eaten then the plant has to branch out and start again. To avoid this waste of energy and time in a short growing season they protect themselves. Some are hairy, many are bitter and some are decidedly poisonous.

# DISTURBED PLACES

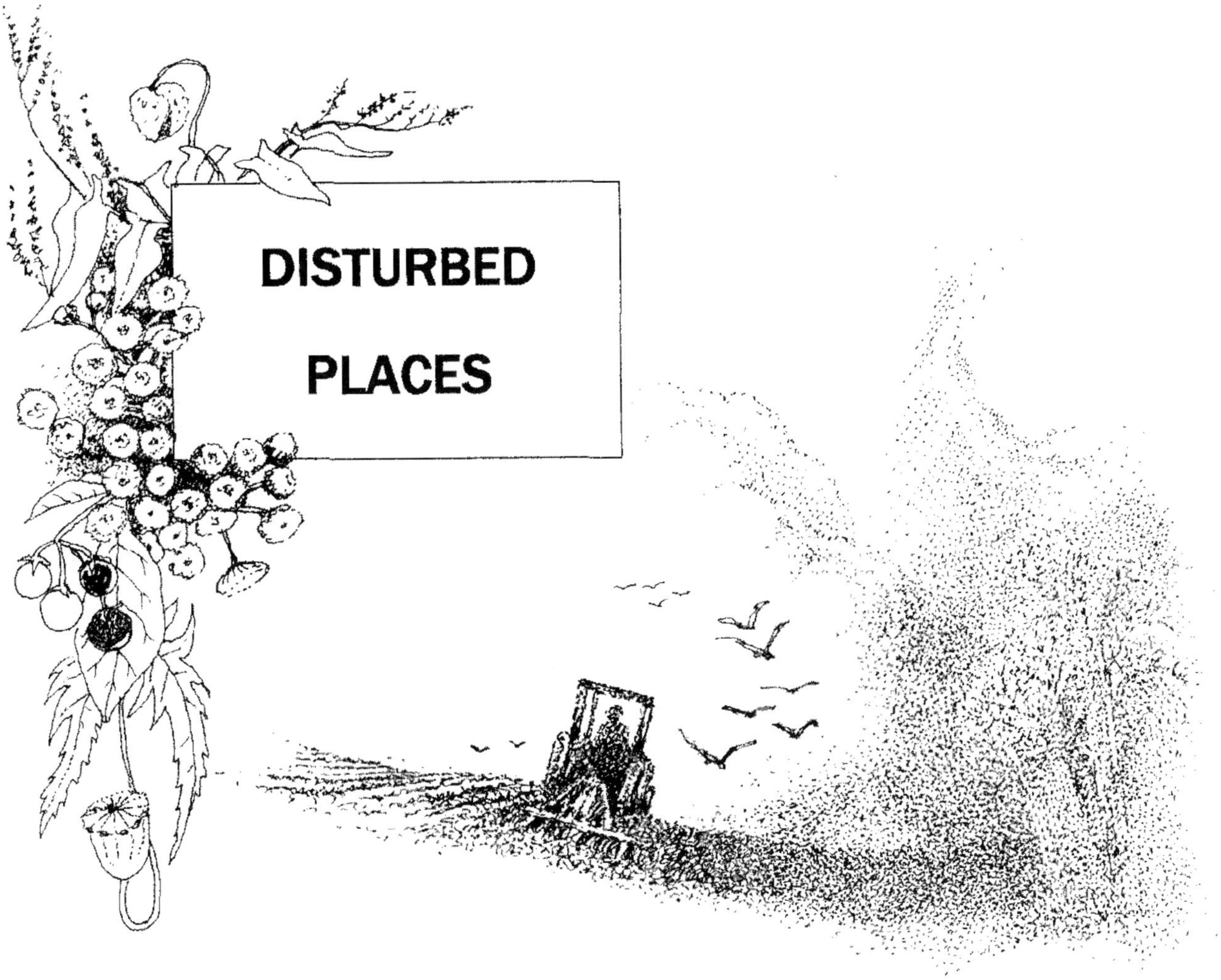

Oh don't the plants like a patch of disturbed soil! Clean up the garden and as soon as you turn back, the weeds pop up again. Farmers get the problem by the acre all across their ploughed fields. Then there are those disturbed areas we prefer to overlook, such as building sites, road schemes, temporary car parks and the like. Seeds will germinate wherever natural disasters, wheels and tools break the soil. Some get despised as 'weeds.' Others please us as 'wild flowers.' Then there are the desirables for which the disturbance was intended, from the crops in the fields to the flowers and vegetables in the garden.

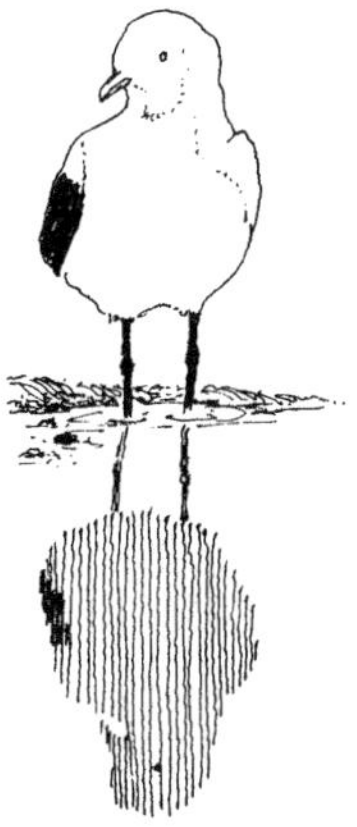

Starting with the crops, anyone would be forgiven for presuming that farmers grow only safe plants but is that so? Apparently not. The poisonous ones are not plants that children need to be taught never to eat but if they are fed in bulk to livestock the situation can be very different. Some of these crops however, such as Oil-seed Rape, can go directly into products on the supermarket shelf and so there are indeed human health concerns. Of course we are told regularly that Britain has the toughest legislation in the world to ensure food safety, which is a comfort at least – but should not be taken as a guarantee. It only reflects our current state of knowledge and practice. We are also told that if coffee and chocolate came up as new products they would not pass the food safety standards.

Potatoes are potentially the most lethal plant in our everyday lives. As science and technology advance so we learn more about the hazards but we also develop new techniques in plant breeding and food processing that may be hazardous in themselves. Time and again questions arise over safety, from genetic engineering to the irradiation of our food – and to put that in a broader context, we all see News items highlighting concerns over the safety of mobile phones, radio masts, overhead power cables etc. Various authorities release the 'all clear' messages, based upon scientific enquiries but these in turn can raise questions about objectivity and selectivity. There are fears that indications of hazards are being suppressed or brushed aside for political and financial reasons or simply ignored as 'not proven'. The trouble with 'not proven' is that for some diseases prevalent today we have no knowledge of what triggers them so there must be missing links. Only a few have been investigated, such as whether potatoes are implicated in spina bifida. More recently contention has arisen over the safety of Rape Oil.

The brassicas are the cabbages and this is a very important family in terms of food production, for both man and beast, since it includes Cabbages, Cauliflowers, Kale, Broccoli, Brussels Sprouts, Mustard, Radish, Rape, Turnips and Swedes, and newer crops to the West such as Pak Choi and Pe Tsai. Older texts will list these as belonging to the Cruciferae family but are now in their own family of Brassicaceae.

**Rape** (*Brassica napus* L.) is not known as an indigenous plant anywhere in the world but is believed to be a fertile hybrid between *Brassica oleracea* (Cabbage) and *B. rapa* (Turnip) and now distinguished as *Brassica napus* ssp *oleifera* DC.). It is believed to have started its crop life thousands of years ago in the Mediterranean region but if the Romans brought it to Britain it died out without trace. The first documentary evidence comes from the 14th century, from the Eastern coastal region, where it had been introduced from over the North Sea. Today it is not popular with the general public. They condemn it as 'new' when patently it is not and condemn its brilliant yellow flowers as 'out of keeping' with the British countryside, when we've grown yellow-flowered crops such as Mustard, Woad and Rape for centuries. Much more understandable are the complaints that it causes hay fever and gives an unpleasant flavour to honey.

After such a long time there is now a number of different strains, under such names as Hungry Gap Kale, Sheep Kale, Rape Kale, Asparagus Kale, etc. Basically they fall into two main groups: those grown for fodder and those grown for their oil-bearing seeds. As a forage crop, Rape is very important. To provide plenty of growth it needs a good, rich soil, which raises questions about how much nitrogen fertilizer is being spread on the land and causing problems to the rest of the environment. Using nitrogen fertilizer should warn the farmer that the crops may be storing up nitrates and Rape is particularly adept at this, particularly at flowering time. This is more likely if the nitrogen fertilizer used was itself nitrates as opposed to urea or ammonium sulphate. When consumed, the nitrates are broken down in the digestive system into ammonia and potentially lethal nitrites. These are absorbed into the bloodstream where they combine with the

oxygen-carrying haemoglobin to form methaemoglobin and that compound will not release oxygen. Death can result in 3-4 hours from oxygen starvation. In milder cases, in cattle, it can affect the storage of vitamin A and lead to problems. When the plant is in bloom it contains sulphur-based heterosides, known also as thiocosides. In Rape they are gluconopine and progoitrine. When these are ingested they yield isothiocyanates which interfere with the functions of the thyroid gland.

Turning to the oil from the seeds, is to turn to an industrial oil, used for example in soap making, lubricants, the base for synthetic rubber, as an enhancer for colour photos in magazines and it is mixed with diesel as a fuel. It does not sound like a food and indeed when there was an expansion in crop production in Britain from the 1960s onwards it was lamented that it could not be used in margarines etc. Science soon got round that! In so doing it has opened up a vast world of controversy, which can be barely touched upon here. They found 'safe' ways of using it in animal feed and it was so used in Britain from 1986 until 1991 when it was banned in Europe because livestock was suffering. Pigs, sheep and cows started to go blind and to develop mental disorders. These disappeared with the withdrawal of the oil from animal feed. Not all scientists were in agreement that Rape oil was the cause. Scientists did find that the oil's content of erucic acid was not desirable – so they bred strains of Rape with low levels and marketed the oil as LEAR (Low Erucic Acid Rape). Better still, from the viewpoint of Big Business, was to get genetic engineers to irradiate the seed and thereby create something with a different genetic make-up, something new, something that was no longer Rape in the strictest sense and so would circumvent restrictive legislation. The new product was developed in Canada and launched as 'Canola Oil' (i.e. Canadian oil) and this is in the foods of some countries. Europe banned GM foods that were not labelled as such, while in Britain consumer power led to supermarkets banning all GM products. Trials of the Rape crop in Britain made headline news as protestors tried to destroy it and campaigned vigorously against the whole idea. Suffice to say at the moment, that Canola Oil, according to the protestors, is not nearly as 'safe' as the industries involved would have us believe – and there are dozens of internet sites extolling its virtues but there are also sites warning what its various constituents can do to us. They make alarming reading but we can be optimistic that with so many billions of dollars invested in this product that the problems will, in due course, be sorted out. Such an important crop is hardly likely to be abandoned altogether. The original Rape seed Oil has been developed, separately from Canola, and is found in foods in Britain. There are medicinal values which lead doctors and nutritionists to recommend it for some people. It is not free of controversy though.

Turning to cereals, these have raised concerns from time to time but are not found to contain active toxic compounds. However, grain can become toxic if it gets infected with fungi, either in the field or after harvesting. There is one member of the grass/cereal family in Britain which has been deemed poisonous and that is Darnel.

**Darnel** (*Lolium temulentum* L.) is a plant of Mediterranean origin that has spread widely round the world as a contaminant of corn. Its dangers have been known since at least the time of the Ancient Greeks and so people sowed it deliberately as an act of malice; the Romans legislated against that, so it must have been quite a regular practice. The most famous account is in the New Testament, as a translation of *tares*:-

"*The kingdom of heaven is likened unto a man which sowed good seed in his field: but while men slept, his enemy came and sowed tares among the wheat, and went his way. But when the blade was sprung up, and brought forth fruit, then appeared the tares also. So the servants of the householder came and said unto him, Sir, didst not thou sow good seed in the field? He said unto them, An enemy hath done this. The servants said unto him, Wilt thou then that we go and gather them up? But he said, Nay; lest while ye gather up the tares, ye root up also the wheat with them. Let both grow together until the harvest. I will say to the reapers, Gather ye together first the tares, and bind them in bundles to burn them: but gather the wheat into my barn.*" (Matthew 13: 25-30 Authorised Version)

Despite this long tradition of being poisonous and of it being the only poisonous grass in Britain, toxicity is still not proven. Some scientific studies have concluded that it is toxic while others vindicate it. Certainly the grass can be infected with a fungus that will produce its own mycotoxins. At present it is not considered a major hazard in Britain, since herbicides have reduced it to a scattered casual of waste places. It is a variable plant with some strains feeling smooth as you run your hand over them while others are coarse and rough; sometimes the seeds heads have awns (bristles) while other strains are without.

The **Buckwheat** (*Fagopyrum esculentum* Moench) is more familiar as a name rather than a plant we would recognise. It was introduced from Asia where it was cropped for its seeds like a cereal. They are rich in fats and albumen but rather 'mealy' for British tastes and so we grew it for pheasant and chicken feed. With the decline in gamekeeping and small-scale poultry rearing the crop has all but disappeared, leaving a few plants to seed around in waste places or to pop up in the garden from seed mixtures for the bird table. Some people grow it to attract bees into the garden for it's a good honey plant and in some countries it is cropped specifically for 'buckwheat honey'.

It belongs to the family Polygonaceae, along with the Docks and Sorrel featured already, and this should warn us the plant might be toxic. Indeed it is. Traditionally, humans have eaten the seeds, safely, since they contain only very low levels of active compounds. Eating the greenery is a different matter. It has been used as fodder but as food for humans it should be taken in small amounts only, as in the bags of mixed 'salad leaves.' Some people are more resistant to its effects than others. It contains two compounds that cause skin to become sensitive to light, with serious consequences.

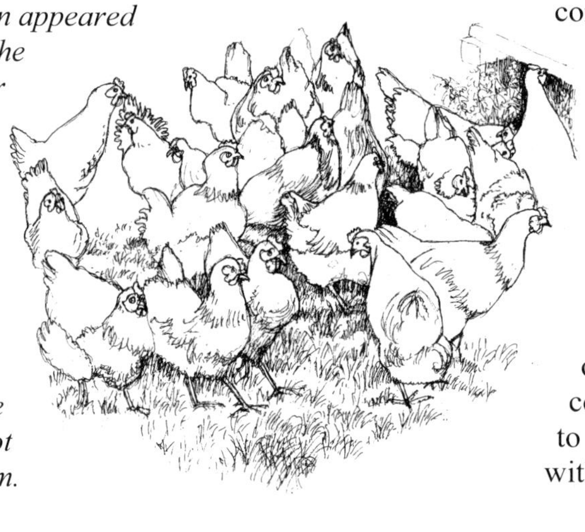

One is fagopyrin, which is specific to this genus and the other is rutin which occurs more widely. Rutin is a flavonol glycoside and when used wisely is valuable as an anti-oxidant and for strengthening veins. It was from Buckwheat that supplies were obtained commercially until richer sources were discovered. Rutin needs treating with respect since it can cause severe photosensitivity in both man and beast. The other toxin in Buckwheat, fagopyrin, gives rise to the condition fagopyrism. The compounds build up under the skin and upon exposure to sunlight they start acting. At first the skin itches and burns, before developing wheals which, in severe cases, result in very nasty ulcers and loss of surface tissues. Sensitivity to pain can increase so that slight knocks are agony. There can be an increased sense of coldness too. Livestock housed permanently indoors do not develop the condition when fed green buckwheat, but should they be exposed to daylight then they certainly do. Bare skin in animals is likely to be in sensitive places such as around the ears, eyes and mouth, making this a particularly distressing condition. Studies of human poisoning have been attributed to an allergic reaction to the compounds rather than any other action of the chemicals. In tests where the allergen was injected the result was sudden death. Take note that window glass and cosmetic preparations that block ultraviolet light are not effective against this type of photosensitivity since it responds to light of different wavelengths.

**Fat Hen** (*Chenopodium album* L) is that tall pale green weed that has a white mealy coating and bolts up in the potato patch and around farmyards, muck heaps etc. It is not likely to have a fan club today but it was valued by our ancestors. Archaeologists find evidence of it in prehistoric cuisines dating as far back as the Bronze Age. Both the leaves and the seeds are nutritious, especially the large knobbly seeds, which are rich in fats and albumen. By the Middle Ages it was known as

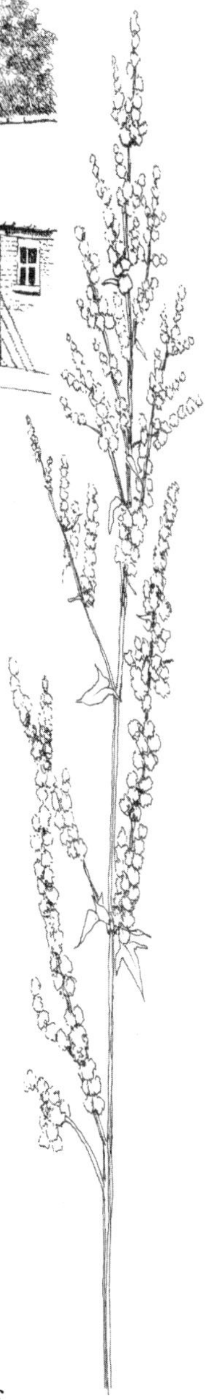

*melde* and is thought to occur in place-names such as Milden in Suffolk, commemorated by a wondrous great iron version as their village sign. In days when so much of the food was cooked in the pot, they were safe since cooking destroys the saponins in the plant which are one of the potential toxins. The human digestive system does not break these down very efficiently so most pass straight through. Oxalic acid is present also and once again cooking reduces the content. Thirdly, the plant accumulates nitrates and when these are digested into nitrites they can be lethal. Accumulations occur during stress conditions such as drought but also when the plant is growing in soils rich in nitrates. This arises nowadays from heavy applications of nitrogen fertilizer but in the past from dunging the land. It grew rampantly as a weed around farms, on middens and dung heaps (hence it being called Dungweed) and through the filthy streets of towns and cities - people earned a living collecting it for market. Fortunately the human digestive system is not very good at breaking down the nitrates into nitrites and so the plant is not as toxic to us as it is to ruminants with their multiple stomachs. Even so, nitrates are implicated in many health problems ranging from gastric cancers to blue-baby syndrome. It sounds as though this plant should be avoided at all costs but if it is cooked and eaten with restraint in a good mixed diet it should be safe. However, the current enthusiasm for eating fresh leaves and the resulting search for variety has led to this being included in 'salad leaves' and again it's important not to eat too many too often. Some people get allergic reactions to handling it and like the Buckwheat it too can cause photosensitisation. On the positive side, it has proven an excellent fattener for poultry ready for the Christmas dinner.

The same can be said for Fat Hen's close relative, **Good King Henry** (*Chenopodium bonus-henricus* L.). It looks similar but is a darker green without the white mealiness. Selected strains for cultivation as a leaf vegetable have much more luxuriant basal arrow-shaped leaves than the weed of farmyards and dung heaps. Its preference for enriched soils means it can absorb high levels of hazardous nitrates. As with Fat Hen it has oxalic acid and saponins and so this should not be eaten to excess, especially as a raw salad herb. Cooking these two plants largely destroys the saponins. If the seeds are being used as a substitute for rice, or mixed with rice, then they should be soaked overnight and thoroughly washed to remove saponins. After such cleaning they can be ground into a meal for mixing with flour.

Now for one of our most colourful weeds, the rare **Corncockle** (*Agrostemma githago* L). This has fine pinkish-purple flowers 3-5cm across, with darker lines on them and a smart white centre, although there can be variation on this. When they were massed amid the ripening corn it must have made a beautiful sight, following on from the main flush of red Corn Poppies or Blind Eyes:- "When the Corn Cockle comes the Blind Eyes go" says our old country lore. It's a thing of the past since the plant is so rare it is generally considered to be extinct in Britain although it is conserved on one site in Norfolk. Elsewhere, we may see it where 'old-fashioned' cornfields have been recreated for historical interest or else grow our own as the seed is readily available at Garden Centres. It is very easy to grow! If the seed pods are not removed they will self-sow into the garden and germinate straight away, to over-winter as seedlings. It was camouflaged with linear leaves just like corn but they are a paler green and hairy. They were also unwelcome. Man has cursed this plant for thousands of years; it is thought to be one of several weeds called 'gith' in the Old Testament, hence 'githago' as its botanical name today. Certainly it is a plant of the Mediterranean basin and is said to have been introduced into Britain by the first farmers 5,000 years ago but archaeologists do not find evidence for it until the Roman period. In the written records of later times we find in farm account books that women were paid for 'cockling' which was to pick it all out of the reaped corn before threshing. The large poisonous seeds might otherwise end up being ground into flour and baked in the bread. Problems like that gave rise to herbicides and seed-cleaning technology, which have banished the Corn Cockle, or at least that is the assumption to explain its disappearance. There are some scientists though who have noted that the historical records show it was most prevalent amid fields of Rye and that it is the decline of Rye that has taken the Corn Cockle with it – indicating that there might be a biological link between the two leading to each associating with the other.

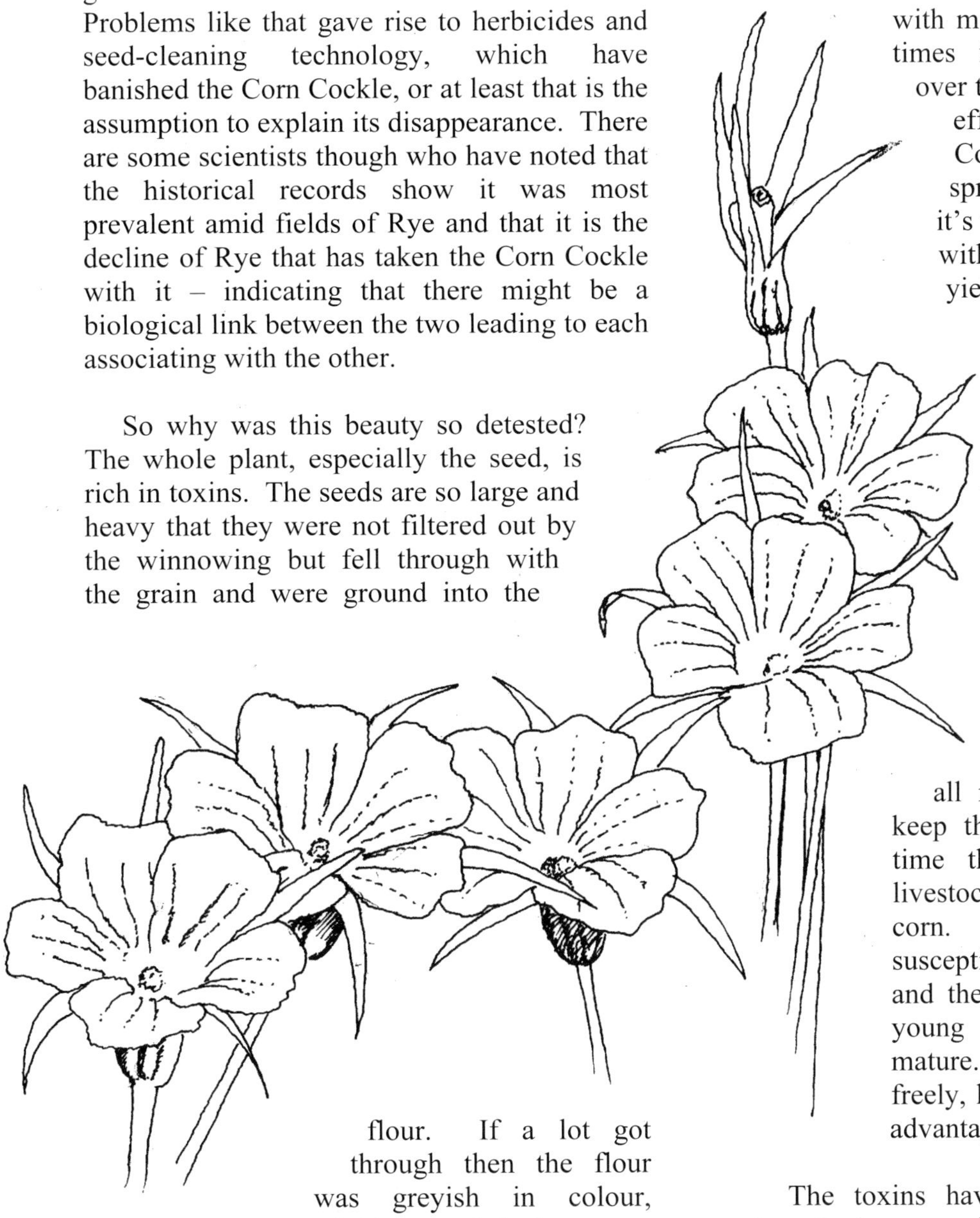

So why was this beauty so detested? The whole plant, especially the seed, is rich in toxins. The seeds are so large and heavy that they were not filtered out by the winnowing but fell through with the grain and were ground into the flour. If a lot got through then the flour was greyish in colour, tasted bitter and had a nasty odour but even a little became a hazard because the toxic effect is cumulative. When the toxins get into the bloodstream (and they are not destroyed by cooking) they attack the red blood cells, causing them to break down (haemolysis) and therefore reducing the blood's capacity to carry oxygen, iron, etc. resulting in debility and anaemia. Over time, death results. Ironically, sufferers were likely to have been fed more of the poison in food, since we are keen to urge the sick to eat: "Got to keep your strength up." Soup has become the stalwart of the anxious carer but if the soup was thickened with flour….! Fortunately if the corn crop was contaminated then all the community started to suffer and so before Old Testament times the 'gith' was identified as the culprit and weeded out. Trampling over the young corn in the autumn was not a bad thing since it produced bushy plants with more seed heads (in modern times farmers dragged a roller over the field to produce just this effect). Some of the Corn Cockle seed waits until the spring to germinate and then it's too late to trample the crop without reducing the potential yield. That's where the 'cockling' ladies enter the picture, spending so much of the winter in the great barns, sitting round on the wooden threshing floor, cleaning the harvest ready to flail it. At least that job sheltered them from the worst of the winter weather but the flailing was back-breaking and considered the worst of all rural tasks, even if it did keep them warm. At the same time they were protecting any livestock that would be fed on the corn. Poultry are the most susceptible (after any carnivores) and then the herbivores, with the young suffering more than the mature. All things that can vomit freely, like man and pigs, are at an advantage.

The toxins have for a long time been described as saponins but for greater accuracy they are colloidal glycosides with the properties of saponins. They are therefore called sapogenins and the version specific to this plant is githagenin. Seeds may contain as much as 5-7% by weight. They produce a wide range of unpleasant, painful and debilitating effects on the body, from mouth to rectum before attacking the rest of the body, including the nervous system, producing tearing pains up the spine. More information on this can be traced under the classification of cerebro-spinal irritants. Incredibly, the seeds have been tried as a coffee substitute –with lethal results.

**Corn Poppies** (*Papaver rhoeas* L.) blazing brilliant red across the fields can spark great affection but staring at them can affect our vision, hence their name Blind Eyes. Apparently this is due to the colour wavelength of that particular red, which upsets our brain's perception after continued stimulation. Red was always the colour of the gods and recurs regularly in our folklore. Thus there is still the belief that poppies in the fields, should be left, *for the good health of the land.* This comes from ancient fertility myths. There is archaeological evidence that these beliefs go right back into prehistoric times, and so for the peoples of the British Isles we do not have the background storyline to the allegory but we do know enough to see parallels at least with the ancient Greek myth to explain the seasons. There we read that Demeter had a beautiful daughter, Persephone, whom the gods spent all day ogling, until Hades could control himself no longer. He burst up out of the Underworld when Persephone was picking poppies in the cornfield and abducted her. Demeter became alarmed when Persephone did not come home for tea and spent days searching for her, in vain. She forbade anything on earth to bear fruit in order to starve everyone into submission. Zeus, the all-seeing one, knew where she was, and relented. He sent Demeter off to the Underworld but then she had to strike a deal with Hades to get her daughter back because Hades had been so enjoying himself 'eating magic pomegranates with her.' They agreed that Demeter could have Persephone back to beautify the upper world for nine months each year but that she had to return to the underworld for the other three. Thus every year the world goes into mourning for the loss of Persephone's beauty for the three months of winter when Demeter had decreed the world would not bear fruit. She promised to lift the ban upon the safe return of her daughter each spring and the poppies are symbolic of this promise, signifying that the earth shall return to good health and bear fruit. Modern science ended that in the mid 20th century with seed cleaning technology and herbicides, although the decline in the use of noxious chemicals in recent years has seen the return of the poppy in some places. That is not a cause for concern in cornfields because seed cleaning removes the poppy seeds from the grain before it gets into our food. In

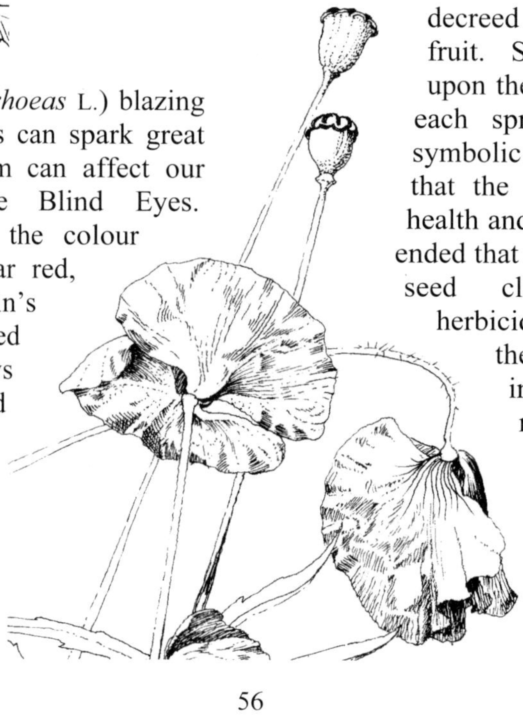

any case, the seeds are supposed to be devoid of toxins although some say they are not. Even so, the cautious admit that we would have to consume 9lb of them before experiencing harmful effects! A few seeds scattered on the bread crust are tasty and safe. However, anybody who is likely to undergo blood tests for opiates should know that an enthusiasm for these flavoursome seeds can produce a positive result in the tests. Remember Corn Poppies are related to the famous Opium Poppy. Our red species is low in toxins although levels rise sharply during flowering and afterwards when the seeds are developing. Thus there is a risk to grazing livestock but ingestion is rarely of such high levels as to cause problems and so poppies are seldom regarded as one of our poisonous plants. At flowering time the petals, containing the non-toxic alkaloid rhoeadine, can be put to use for making a pain killer. They are macerated in pure organic olive oil, in clear glass bottles, and put in sunlight for several weeks, during which time the rhoeadine separates out and can be used pharmaceutically. The resulting painkiller acts fast and is very effective. We turned to this during the Second World War when so many medical supplies were needed. County committees, of botanists and flower-lovers, were set up and trained to ensure they really did know their plants before they were sent off to gather wild medicinal herbs (about nine species) and poppy petals were one of the things they had to collect.

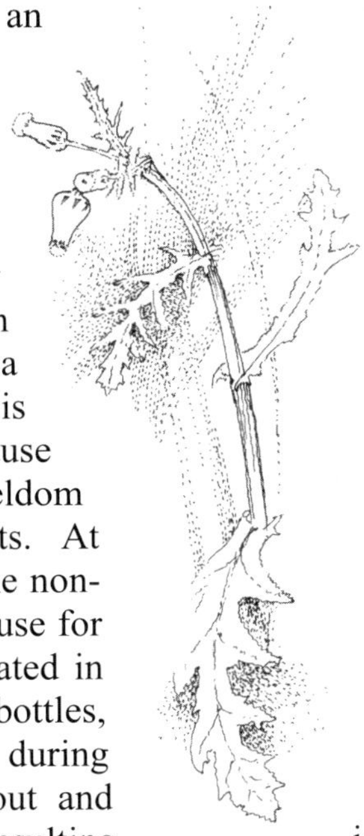

Let's go to the other extreme now and focus on a little weed with tiny yellow flowers; at least it's usually small but if it likes your growing conditions can exceed a foot high. The **Groundsel** (*Senecio vulgaris* L.) will be very familiar to many gardeners, especially those with vegetable plots that inevitably have areas of bare soil from time to time. Up comes the Groundsel as if by magic. Farmers can get it by the acre! Its name comes from the Saxon *grundeswylge,* meaning 'pus-swallower' from its use as a dressing for abcesses. That got changed to *grundeswylige* meaning 'ground-swallower' from this ability to mass invade disturbed soil. The original reminds us that Groundsel has been featured in herbalism for over two thousand years of written records and obviously long before that too. However, encouragements to eat it should be ignored. When the keeping of budgerigars was so fashionable, owners were told to provide their birds with a bit of groundsel. They loved it. There have also been encouragements to chop it up and add it to our salads (once tried, never forgotten, as far as I'm concerned; mine goes straight into the compost bin). Well a little bit now and again may be safe but note that this weed and the seven other Groundsels in Britain belong to the genus *Senecio* and are therefore *very* close relatives of the deadly Ragwort. Groundsel also contains pyrrolizidine alkaloids of Ragwort fame, namely senecionine, seneciphylline, retrorsine, riddelline, intergerrimine, spartioidine, and usaramine), which is a couple fewer than Ragwort, but enough to warn us. They will still cause irreversible liver damage. The effects are cumulative and so small amounts over a sustained period can still be fatal and is the commonest scenario. Some countries, therefore, have concerns that the seeds (and even the greenery) may get harvested with food crops, such as grain, and end up in the flour. Tests have proved positive. In Britain, herbicides are used by our farmers to control weeds such as these. Groundsel can be a menace to British farmers if it gets into fodder crops such as Alfalfa/Lucerne (*Medicago sativa*) and even drying it into hay will not destroy the alkaloids. In the past of course it was standard practice to turn the livestock onto the land to eat the weeds after the harvest, which raises the question as to how often plants with slow cumulative toxins, such as *Senecio* and *Rumex,* were responsible for livestock losses. Time and again records report that livestock were stricken with 'murrain' and died. Nobody has ever ascertained exactly what was meant by 'murrain'; it could easily be these types of food poisoning, especially as the effects can take weeks or even months to show and their cause and effect can be distanced beyond recognition.

Ah, now for the **Hemlock** (*Conium maculatum* L.) famous as an agent of death since ancient times. With a drink of this herb Socrates was killed in 399 BCE when he was sentenced to death for impiety. What ensued was recorded by Plato:- "*He walked about and, when he said his legs were heavy, lay down on his back, for such was the advice of the attendant. The man who had administered the poison laid his hands on him and after a while examined his feet and legs, then pinched his foot hard and asked if he felt it. He said "No"; then after that, his thighs; and passing upwards in this way he showed us that he was growing cold and rigid. And again he touched him and said that when it reached his heart, he would be gone... To this question he made no reply, but after a little while he moved; the attendant uncovered him; his eyes were fixed.*" (Plato, *Euthyphro, Apology, Crito, Phaedo*)

Today some toxicologists refute that these are the symptoms of Hemlock poisoning, but true or not, they are a graphic reminder to treat this plant with respect. It is a biennial that grows up from a swollen tap root that resembles a parsnip and has been eaten as such, with fatal results. It belongs to the carrot family and has the same cut leaves of a delicate ferniness but lax, responding to the breezes and so glossy they can reflect the blue of the sky. Up grow straight stems, often taller than ourselves, with the usual flat white umbrella flowers of this family. Many people find these species very confusing and even a good drawing would need to be read very carefully, so simply look at the stems. Look for purple spots, supposedly the blood of Socrates, for this is the only member of this family that you will find so spotted. Even if you find a puny little specimen the purple spots will warn you that it is indeed the Hemlock. It is not a good idea to handle it but when bruised it emits an unpleasant odour reminiscent of mice (emanating from the toxin coiine which gives also its bitter taste). Often many plants germinate in a patch of disturbed soil to produce a small plantation, frequently where there have been roadworks and along motorways.

Hemlock contains a whole cocktail of dangerous alkaloids, with coniceine greatest in the fresh state but this level drops on drying, leaving coniine as the prime agent. Other compounds have been isolated and named conhydrine, lambda-coniceine, N-methylconiine and pseudoconhydrine etc. The most dangerous is usually reckoned to be coiine (a piperidine alkaloid, 2-propylpiperidine), which is a neurotoxin that alters normal brain function. Thus Plato described the body of Socrates steadily closing down, till it finally reached the heart and respiratory system. It affects both man and beasts but fortunately rather a lot of greenery needs consuming before livestock die; some 4-5 lb for a horse, down to half a pound for a sheep. At first they tremble and become agitated before going into a depressed state as their bodies start to close down. This can last for hours, sometimes followed by a surprising recovery (although females may later deliver young with birth defects). Should the dose be too great then death from respiratory failure occurs after 5-10 hours. The greatest concentrations of toxins are in the roots and seeds and this is where fatalities in man occur, from eating the roots and mistaking the seed for Fennel. Children have died after using the hollow stems as pea-shooters.

The plant's ability to numb the brain has led to this herb being used as a pain-killer and sedative for centuries, in European and Arab cultures. Nowadays it is used less because it is so dangerous and can lead to birth defects. It has been reviewed as a source of anti-cancer drugs since it has a long history for that purpose in folk medicine, particularly for breast cancer. Other traditional uses included treatments for arteriosclerosis, arthritis, dizziness, epilepsy, haemorrhoids, insomnia, liver diseases, mastitis, nervous conditions, prostate problems, rabies, skin disorders, whooping cough and as an antidote for strychnine poisoning or to calm sexual urges. Do not try home remedies as this plant is very dangerous. Treat with extreme caution the beliefs that the plant is less toxic in cooler climates, or in the south rather than the north of England, and ignore the notion that heat destroys the poison so it's safe as a cooked vegetable.

**Tansy** (*Tanacetum vulgare* L) has beautiful jagged cut leaves and produces heads of bright gold buttons in high summer but if you go to pick some you'll find it incredibly tough and smelly. When fresh it smells somewhat minty but the pleasance soon wears off! People used to rub Tansy into meat to keep the flies off and it was rubbed into corpses for the same reason and to repel worms after burial. Intestinal worms were voided with Tansy tea. Gerard tells us it was strewn among clothes as a deodoriser, leaving us to wonder just how bad those Elizabethan clothes smelt if Tansy was an improvement! It is said the smell puts animals off grazing it but the information available is contradictory, in terms of which animals will or will not eat it. Our ancestors used it for hundreds of years, for cosmetic, medicinal and culinary purposes. . Back in the Middle Ages people preferred strongly flavoured food and Tansy certainly provided that, together with a bitterness that contrasted with their other flavourings. From the 15th to the 19th centuries a 'tansye' was an omelette, especially a bitter one. It had been promoted by the Pre-Reformation Catholic Church during Lent, as one of the five bitter herbs used to commemorate the Passover. So Tansy Cakes or Tansies (the omelette) became widespread fare at Easter. People grew it in their gardens as a free alternative to the higher class nutmeg or cinnamon, which were expensive imports. In the 17th century Isaac Walton, of angling fame, loved a tasty dish of minnows fried in egg yolk, with flowers of Primrose and Cowslip and a sprinkling of Tansy. It became an officially recognised flavouring in the British Pharmacoeia until about 1990 when it was recommended for withdrawal, as we became more aware of its toxic effects. Nevertheless it is still used but if old recipes are being followed the Tansy should be replaced with another bitter herb such as Tarragon. Certainly do not consume a lot of Tansy tea since that has proved fatal in the United States. Do not use it at all when the consumer has epilepsy as Tansy can trigger convulsions from which deaths have resulted, nor is it safe for any pregnant consumer as it affects the uterine muscles and causes bleeding. It's best left as a garden ornamental, although it runs about a bit with its long stolons. Even there beware of handling it too much since there are indications that its toxic oil can be absorbed through the skin. The prime toxin is thujone, which is a terpenoid ketone, and exists in two forms. It takes its name from the genus *Thuja* that gives us the familiar hedging conifers and it occurs also in Junipers and Cedars and such herbaceous plants as *Artemesia.* The name *Tanacetum* derives from the Greek word 'thanatos' – from the god of death.

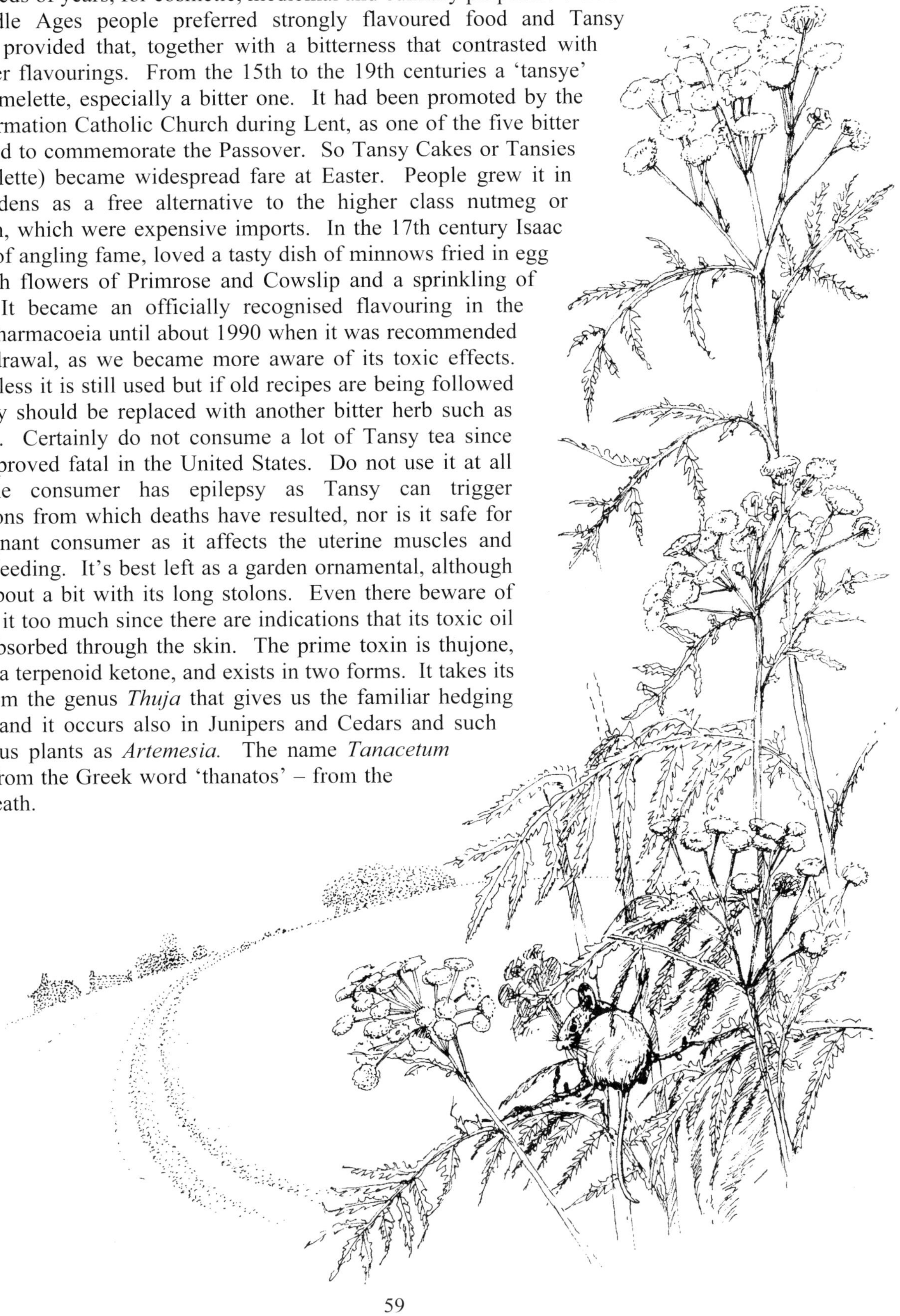

**Deadly Nightshade** (*Atropa belladonna* L) is a good starting point for this section since so many people have heard of it. Not enough people are wary of it – it is one of Europe's major causes of death due to plant poisoning. Let us start then with tuition in recognising the plant. It is a perennial, so you might come across very young plants with only a single stem a few centimetres high, or you might find a mature specimen, several years old, that has grown into a large clump, up to two metres high. The crucial point is the leaves. They grow up the stem in pairs, with the peculiarity that one is much bigger than the other – often two thirds bigger. Their juice smells unpleasant but do not handle them since the toxins can be absorbed through the skin. The flowers are single bells growing in the leaf axil, and are a distinctive purplish green, in my experience. Some books say "lurid violet or greenish" or "brownish purple" but some of the photographs on the Internet show reddish blooms (maybe that is due to the colour processing or perhaps the subject was a foreign specimen). The blooms are about 2cm long and begin in June and run on into September, followed by berries which are particularly noticeable when their greenness ripens to a very glossy black. They are the size of a small cherry. These are attractive to children but there was a News item recently of an adult couple who had collected them during a walk on the South Downs, popped them in the freezer and later made a fruit pie out of them. After two days the neighbours missed them. When the house was entered the couple were found unconscious but still alive. The wonders of modern science applied skilfully in the Intensive Care Unit restored the couple to health with no apparent long-lasting affects. Amazing. Take care not to be the next News item. Be particularly wary on alkaline soils, whether chalk or limestone, primarily in central and southern England, but it does occur more widely, including Ireland. It is not common, and is becoming increasingly rare, but if you find one you may well find others in the vicinity.

The whole plant is poisonous, from the roots to the berries and even though the concentrations of toxins vary through the different parts of the plant there is no part that is safe. If you think an adult has eaten a berry do not panic; it is usually said that up to three berries can be consumed safely but not if it's a child. These toxins go under various names but here we are interested in the three prime alkaloids, atropine, hyoscyamine and scopolamine , with the spotlight here resting upon atropine which takes its name from the genus of the Deadly Nightshade, *Atropa.* That was taken from the Greek Fate, Atropos, who wielded the shears that cut the thread of life. Before Tudor times this plant was known as **Dwale**. Isn't that a wonderful gloomy, sinister, sounding name, evoking the twilight state of mind that consumers can fall into? Within thirty minutes of consumption some, or all, of the

following affects can be experienced:-dilated pupils, dry eyes, dry mouth, dry skin, loss of voice, nausea, vomiting, depression, increased heart rate, muscle failure, delirium, exhaustion, hallucinations, general paralysis, coma, death due to respiratory failure. This is not a plant to take chances with – atropine is so powerful that one investigation found that one part of atropine in 130,000 parts of water was still enough to dilate the pupils of a cat's eyes. Dogs and cats are particularly susceptible so mind little children do not feed the berries to their dog on a country walk. We would imagine that these toxins originated to deter grazing but livestock does not seem to be at a particular risk. There are reports of large amounts (several kilograms) being consumed by horses and cattle without ill effect. Indeed it is said that rabbits, sheep and goats are not affected at all, and birds eat the berries without observable repercussions. However, it should be removed from pastures grazed by animals destined for the meat market since the atropine persists in muscle tissue and can render the meat toxic.

It's not all gloom and doom. Man has always been fascinated by this herb and has used it for thousands of years, as a poison, as a hallucinogen, as a pain-killer, and as an ingredient in witches' flying ointments. There has been a continuum of attempts to find ways of using it to our advantage in medicine. It was being investigated as soon as scientific advances allowed and was isolated in 1809 by Philipp Lounz Geiger (1785-1803) and his assistant Germaine Henri Hess (1802-1850). Then began the long and continuing story of exploring its potential in medicine. Back in the Renaissance, ladies dripped Deadly Nightshade juice into their eyes to make the pupils dilate to make the ladies look more attractive – hence the name Belladonna, beautiful lady. Now atropine was seen as a way of enlarging the pupil to our allow doctors to see into the eye better while slightly stronger doses paralyse the eye muscles completely ready for surgery. Furthermore, atropine switches off our bodily secretions including the tear glands and so the eyes do not water. Stronger doses put people into "twilight sleep" and that was crucial in the development of anaesthesia - see the work of John Snow (1813-1858). Put that with its pain-killing effects and muscle relaxation and gynaecologists were interested in the possibility of using it to ease difficult births. As the science of anaesthesia progressed they found some drugs had undesirable side-effects that atropine did not exhibit and that is still true today. The drug is still important to the anaesthetist, especially in the premedication. By switching off the body's secretions it reduces the risk of fluid blocking the airways and its ability to relax muscles includes the bronchial muscles which again aids the anaesthetist in his crucial work of controlling the body's reactions during a procedure. Out in the Accident and Emergency area it is employed again. It can be used to counteract the effects of other poisons, for which in some cases we have no other option. This has included treatment for a nerve gas developed in Germany during the Second World War, but fortunately never used. The continuing threat of chemical warfare means supplies of atropine are quietly monitored and transported to war zones.
Chemical warfare upon insects is considered crucial to the world's crop production but many insecticides affect humans too and so it is atropine that has been found effective to try and save victims of exposure to organophosphate insecticides, such as parathion. The arguments over organophosphates continue and so does the work with atropine. There are programmes of selective breeding etc. to produce new strains of super-toxic plants and countries like the United States grow fields of Deadly Nightshade for the pharmaceutical industries. We may see such fields in Britain as farmers seek new ways to try and earn a living off their land. They've started already with Opium Poppies.

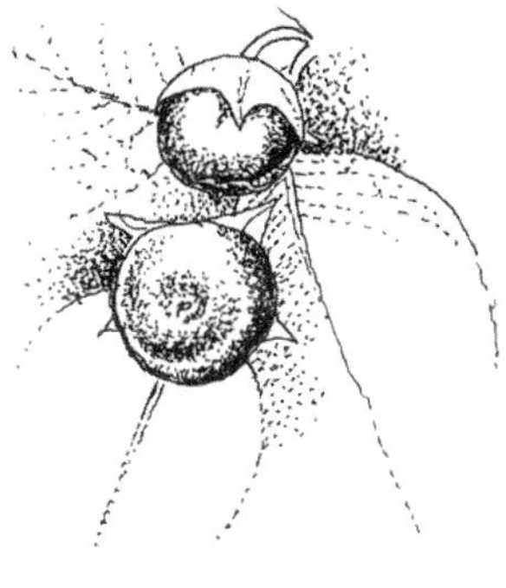

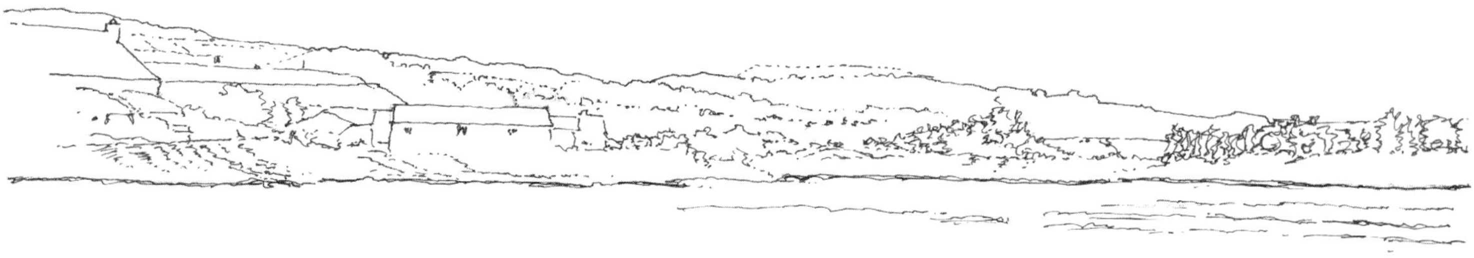

**Henbane** (*Hyoscyamus niger* L.) insured that prehistoric man communed with his gods. It's one of our most powerful hallucinogenic herbs and has been used since Neolithic times, at least. Evidence gets unearthed by the archaeologists – one broken piece of pot can tell us so much. The residue remaining from the last contents can be analysed and identified. From the potsherd itself we can judge the size of the vessel and putting this evidence together leads us to realise that some of the large pots were used for brewing. When Henbane is present we realise that this was a brew drugged with herbs that would have given hallucinations and out-of-world experiences. Suddenly those silent sentinel stones of our prehistoric tombs and monuments take on a new life, as we imagine the music and singing and dancing of the assembled, high on drugs, possibly enhanced by burning Henbane seeds in the incense mixture. Of course we don't know whether such brews were restricted to the shaman or whether it was shared with the assembly as part of the ritual, like the wine at the Christian Eucharist ritual today. We do not know how such societies were structured so we do not know whether the brewer was a specialist or whether he called upon a specialist herbalist for his drugs but we do know that herbs like Deadly Nightshade and Henbane were absent from Scotland until man got there. Spilt seed could have started off the herbs in the wild there but so too could deliberate cultivation. The Neolithic peoples were our first farmers so if they could cultivate field crops why not a herb patch? Again, we don't have the evidence, yet. Henbane, in this context, begs to be cultivated simply because it is an annual or biennial. There's no option of leaving a clump in a corner to harvest year after year, like the perennial Deadly Nightshade. Seed must be saved and sowed, unless it naturalised fast and produced enough supplies. That might have been possible since each plant can produce anything up to half a million seeds per season and so few are needed per person at any one time, to get the desired effects. Nevertheless it does suggest there was something akin to trade in this commodity although it must have been a much commoner plant in times past since there's a flea beetle (*Pyslliodes hyoscyami*) that has evolved a dependence upon it, which could never have happened if Henbane was a great rarity.

Oh if only we could go back and see the great Bronze Age ritual centres in use! Of course we can get ideas (and they are only ideas, not evidence) from later times. Most famous are probably the 'orgies' at the Oracle of Delphi. From the behavioural descriptions, toxicologists can deduce which drugs were having powerful effects and Henbane featured prominently. It stayed in brews right through the Middle Ages. It was crucial in giving flavour and effect in the original Pilsen beer. Pilsen derives from *Bilson / Bilsenkraut*, the German word for Henbane. (The connection with the town of Pilsen came later). This usage was outlawed by the Bavarian Purity Law of 1516 but elsewhere Henbane remained in some beers until the 20th century.

Look for Henbane in disturbed soils, whether sandy or chalky, where there's a tilth in which the seeds can get established quickly. It is resistant to salt spray and is recorded from many locations around the coastline. Once the Normans had introduced rabbits it took a liking to the loose soil they scrape up but since myxomatosis in the 1950s rabbits have ceased to be the great burrowers and scratchers of before and Henbane has declined. It produces a basal crown of deeply cut smelly leaves and then it shoots up about a metre with bell-shaped flowers in the leaf axils. These twist up and round till they look like a single line up the stem. They are beautiful. Each has a pale base colour, ranging from yellowish through to lilac, overlaid with purple veins. The seed capsules can each produce about 500 tiny

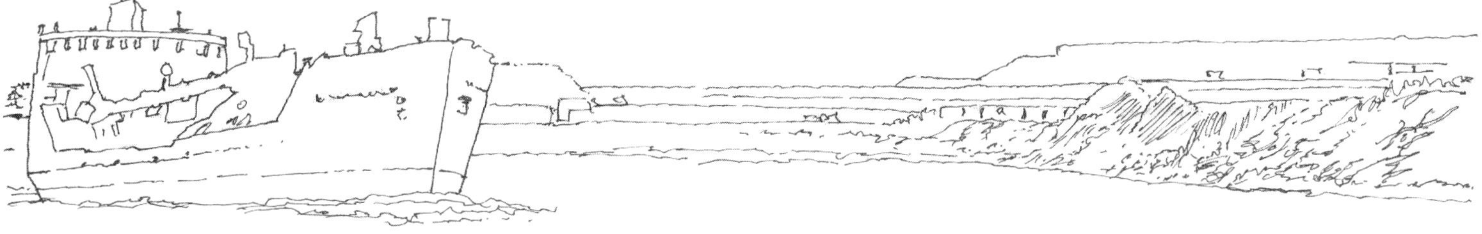

seeds. The whole plant is toxic so livestock should not be allowed to graze it. It is not as poisonous as Deadly Nightshade, which contains ten times as much alkaloid, but it still takes only a few of the tiny seeds to bring on the symptoms of poisoning in a child. Its reputation as a killer has probably been exaggerated by a few high-profile stories whether in Shakespeare's *Hamlet* or its use by Dr Crippen to murder his wife in 1910. The drugs involved are primarily the aforementioned alkaloids, atropine and scopolamine, with its own forms of the latter, known as hyoscyamine and hyoscine. Fortunately, the plant is smelly, which deters people from picking and eating it but there are reports of fatalities from eating the large roots. The seeds enable a much more careful dosage and have been important to man for medicine as well as ritual. Taken at rituals it would have increased the sense of excitement by giving a dry mouth, increased heart rate and greater sense of light as the pupils dilate, with blurred vision and giddiness. Then a delirious frenzy develops, leading to hallucinations. After that, continued inhalation or consumption really brings on the trouble, with delirium, coma and death. Although we can read descriptions, that sound quite exciting, of the ancient Classical rituals, with the priests and priestesses communing with their gods, this is a dangerous herb containing highly toxic drugs and should not be used for experiments. In skilled hands it has high medicinal value. Many of you readers will have benefited from Henbane in the premedication received before an operation because hyoscyamine has a sedative effect upon the central nervous system. It relaxes muscles too and so it has been very successful in treating tremor and rigidity of the muscles in the early stages of Parkinson's Disease. Many readers will have administered the drug themselves by giving motion-sickness tablets to children. It has been used as a painkiller, in preference to opium because it does not cause constipation.

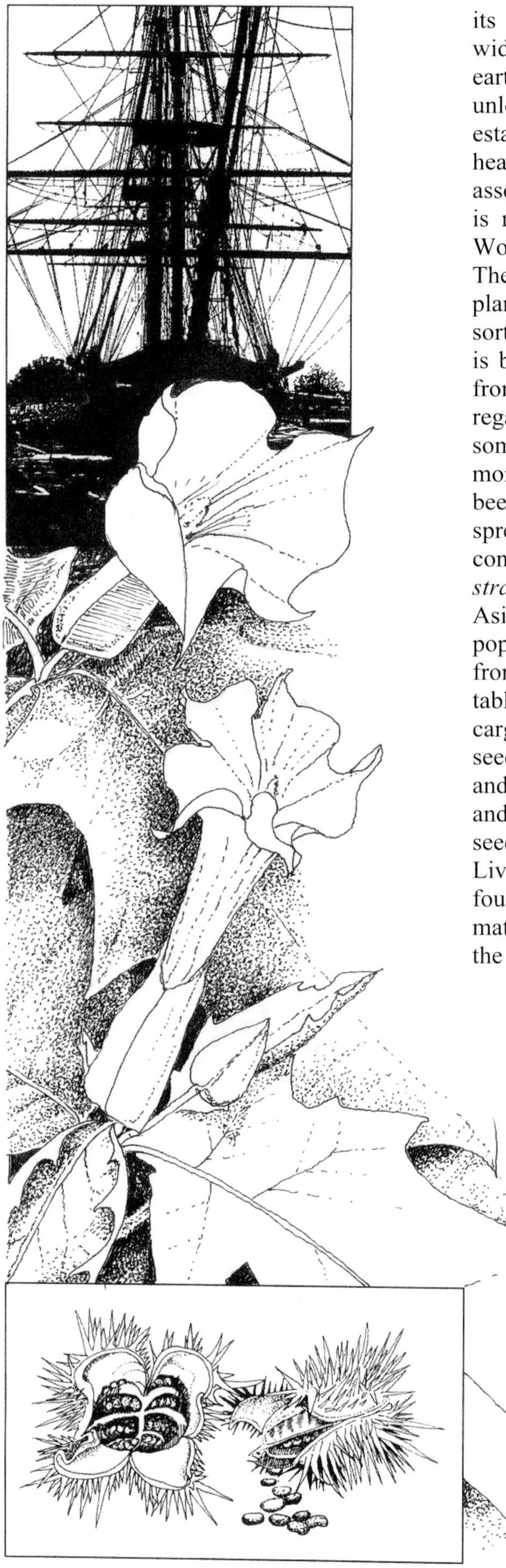

**Thornapple** (*Datura stramonium* L.) spent much of its life sailing round the world, judging from its widespread distribution. Its seeds got mixed into the earth used as ballast in sailing ships, to be loaded and unloaded at far-flung docks where it was able to establish itself. It loves the rich loose soil of rubbish heaps (hence illus next page) and middens so it is always associated with man but whence did it originate? There is no clear answer to that but evidence suggests Old World rather than New, and Asia rather than Europe. The name may help, for when Linnaeus classified the plants in the 18th century he took what had become a sort of international name, Datura, for the genus. Datura is believed, by some, to come from the Hindi *dhatura*, from the Sanskrit *d'hustura*, which led to India being regarded as the place of origin. The name is *tatorah* in some languages of Eastern India. However, there is more than one species and since ancient times they have been important in medicine, which also helped their spread. If it all started in India then probably the species concerned was *Datura fastuosa* rather than *D. stramonium*. The latter possibly came from Western Asia, from the regions around the Caspian Sea. Now it pops up in my garden every year. I suspect it comes from the birdseed mixtures used on the neighbours' bird-tables but it has come into the country with a variety of cargoes. In my childhood it was a contaminant of Kale seed and it was my Saturday morning job to go through and weed it out before the electric fence was moved up and the cattle allowed to feed on the next strip. Modern seed-cleaning technology has wiped out that problem. Livestock are not very fond of it anyway because of its foul odour, with which it presumably has a taste to match (slugs and snails love it though). In some parts of the country it is called Stinkweed or Stinkwort.

Thornapple contains tropanes, which are among the most virulent toxins in the plant world. Thornapple has its own variations, such as daturine and metaloidine, although there is more of the latter in other species. It is grown in Europe as a source of hyoscyamine. These compounds are once again sedative and muscle relaxant drugs, used nowadays for example, in controlling the effects of Parkinson's Disease. However, this is not a plant to try for home medication. It is particularly dangerous because there is an enormous variation in its potency – nobody can tell how much is safe to use. Furthermore, the tolerance level of our bodies towards this herb is especially low and severe effects can set in after thirty minutes.

Fortunately it is still not a common plant since the seed does not germinate until the warm weather arrives but if climate change gives us longer, hotter summers then it could thrive, as it does in the summers of the United States. There, sadly, it has become a major hazard to young Americans who try exploiting its hallucinogenic properties as a recreational drug, with disastrous and often lethal results. It is particularly sad since casualties who survive invariably report that the experience was totally unpleasant. This is definitely not a 'joy weed' and there is no antidote. Survivors are liable to suffer from lasting depression for up to a year, blurred vision that lasts for weeks or months, and loss of short term memory for weeks. The hallucinations are particularly dangerous because users do not know that they are hallucinating. They cannot distinguish between reality and hallucination. To them it is all real. So witches using it in their 'flying ointments' were certain they flew and priests really believed the gods had spoken to them. It may sound fun but remember that users don't report enjoying it.

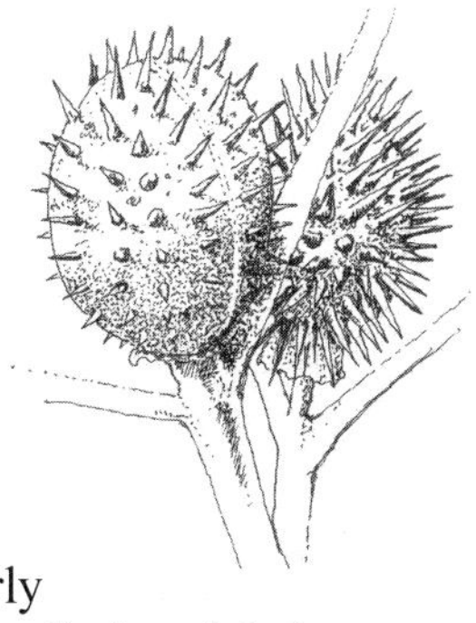

It is very distinctive. The stem produces a terminal white trumpet flower which does not always open but can remain spiral-closed. There is a rich scent to attract small night-flying moths for pollination but large moths, like hawk-moths, and honey bees are all affected by the toxins. Inhale the scent as little as possible. The stem bifurcates on either side of this bloom to produce two more and so forth until there is a fine structured plant, with dark green leaves that are deeply cut. Look to levels lower than the blooms and there in the joints will be the sharp-spined fruits that give it the name Thornapple. They will grow to about 5cm across and remain green as they split open to reveal four compartments, filled with large blackish-brown seeds that are ridged to grip the soil. They can remain viable in the soil for a long time, awaiting suitable conditions to germinate but never in shade. It is available for garden use, where it can make a good spot plant up to a metre high, but think carefully if little children use your garden and do not plant it where visitors can stop to enjoy the scent.

Thornapple has another popular name in America, **Jimsonweed,** which is a contraction of Jamestown Weed. There, in 1676, British soldiers were trying to quell the Rebellion of Bacon but the colonists adulterated the soldiers' meal with Thornapple. What ensued was recorded in 1705 by Robert Beverly in *The History and Present State of Virginia.* Many garbled versions are in circulation today so here is what he wrote:-

*"a very pleasant comedy, for they turned natural fools upon it for several days: one would blow up a feather in the air; another would dart straws at it with much fury; and another, stark naked, was sitting up in a corner like a monkey, grinning and making mows at them; a fourth would fondly kiss and paw his companions, and sneer in their faces with a countenance more antic than any in a Dutch droll.*

*In this frantic condition they were confined, lest they should, in their folly, destroy themselves – though it was observed that all their actions were full of innocence and good nature. Indeed they were not very cleanly; for they would have wallowed in their own excrements, if they had not been prevented. A thousand such simple tricks they played, and after 11 days returned themselves again, not remembering anything that had passed."*

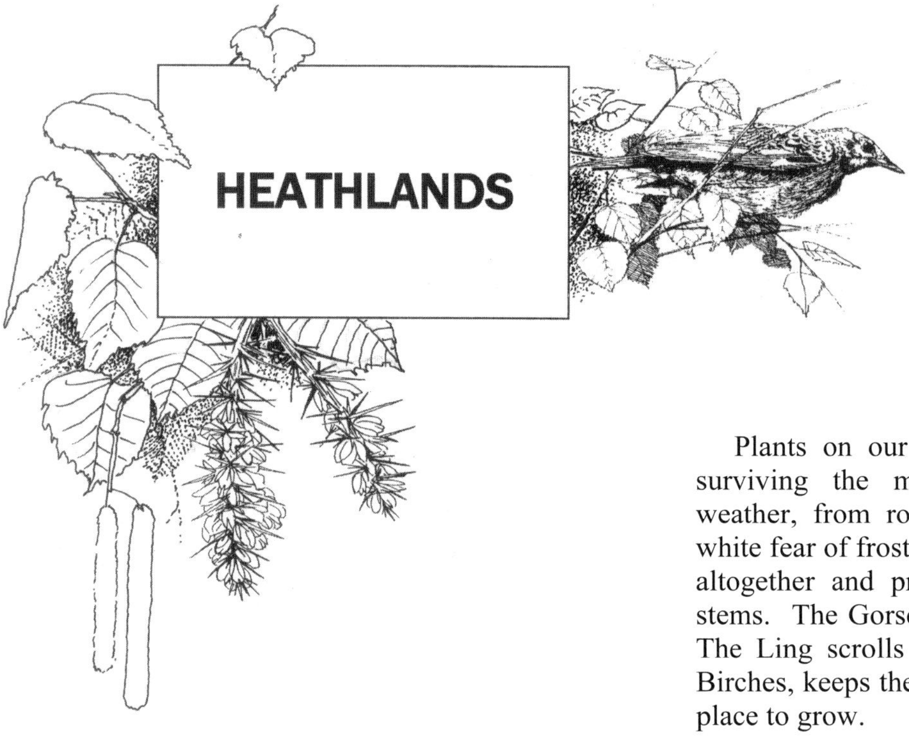

# HEATHLANDS

Plants on our heathlands are adapted for surviving the meanest soils and bullying weather, from rock-cracking sunshine to the white fear of frost. The Broom sheds its leaves altogether and produces food through green stems. The Gorse turns its leaves into spines. The Ling scrolls up its leaves, and with the Birches, keeps them small. It's an unforgiving place to grow.

Heathlands are beautiful sanded landscapes to explore, where Pine mingles with Birch, heather with bracken, Gorse with Broom and there's another range of beauties to find in the wet areas. The **Birches** (*Betula* spp.) are not well defended against attack and so support the third greatest number of insects on the trees of Britain. Even so, we get a hint that there are active compounds from its traditional use in Birch Tar Soap. The natural antiseptic is important in horse racing where the fences have always been constructed from Birch but when the great age of plastics burst upon us it was decided to replace natural Birch with a more resistant plastic version. Then the trouble started. The twigs scratched the horses' legs and the wounds became infected which had never happened with natural Birch. Fences are now once again constructed from natural Birch and the problem has gone away. The trees are not so toxic as to be a hazard and so wines on the market made from the sap, bark, etc. are safe. There is one notable exception and that is the North American **Sweet** or **Cherry Birch** (*Betula lenta* L.) that may be encountered in gardens and tree collections, for the sake of its black-brown bark. Its oil contains methyl salicylate, as per other Birches, but at a level that means absorbing even small amounts can be lethal. However, it is a valuable compound, being used commonly in medicine and is familiar to many from its use as 'oil of wintergreen'.

*(Heathland illus. left: courtesy of Janet Blight)*

**Broom** (*Cytisus scoparius* L.) can be found in sunny places among the trees but withstands the open heaths admirably. Formerly it was used as animal fodder, probably most often in the winter when the young stems remain green and nutritious. They taste bitter as a warning and in small doses stimulate the bodily systems as a tonic during a boring regimen of hay. It contains the quinolizidine alkaloid sparteine (and isosparteine) which affects the electro-conductivity of the heart muscle, affecting its rhythms, which can be dangerous. The compound can also interact with cardiac medicines. People with cardiac problems should avoid consuming this plant, including wine made from the flowers since the toxins are found in the flowers as well as the rest of the plant. In the past these have been added to beer to increase its intoxicating effects. Those who are pregnant should avoid Broom since the sparteine stimulates uterine contractions and was used officially for this during the 1970s. It was soon discontinued due to the toxic side effects. Broom increases urination also and has been used as a diuretic, the action being attributed to the compounds scoparin or scoparoside. Further research is still needed before we can understand fully the toxicity of this plant so be wary of it. Broom seeds can occur as substitutes for hops, coffee and capers and in some herbal medicines.

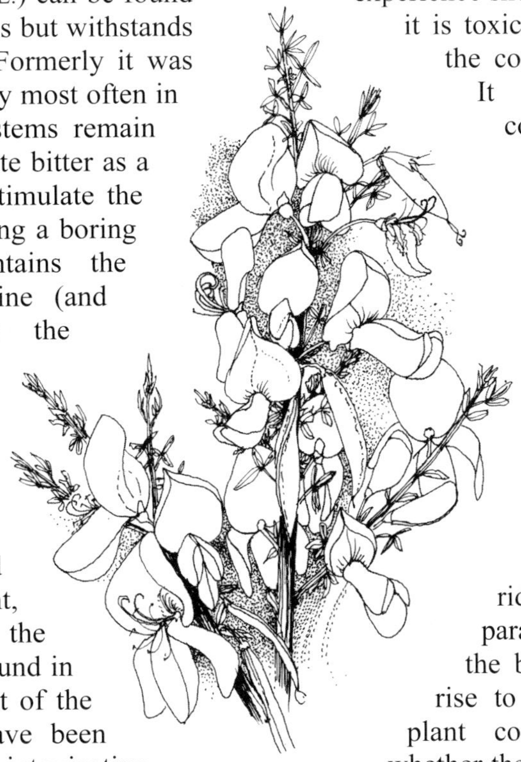

We know even less about Broom's close relation, the sharp-spined **Gorse** (*Ulex europaeus* L.). This too is a plant of the open heathlands but can be found among trees where it has been overtaken by invading scrub. With such spines it hardly needs chemical defences at all but in its youngest stage the stems grow up soft and spineless and have leaves. Thus it used to be sown with corn to provide fodder when the livestock were turned onto the stubble after the harvest. By now experience should have taught us whether it is toxic, since it contains some of the compounds found in Broom. It has not caused major concerns, which should have become apparent since it was formerly fed to horses in large quantities (about 40 lb per day per average sized farm horse). It does not appear to be dangerous. Indeed, there is a tradition among some horse-owners, in the New Forest and other heathland areas, that feeding Gorse to horses rids their stomachs of parasites and worms, especially the bot worm. This has given rise to debate as to whether the plant contains an insecticide or whether the worms are removed by the abrasive nature of the fodder.

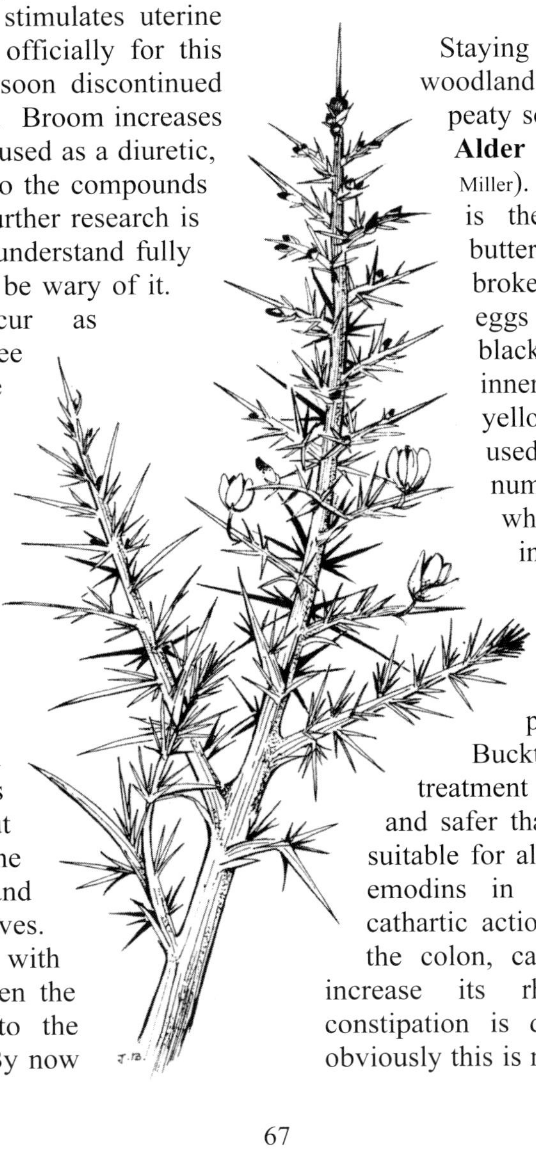

Staying with trees but moving into woodland edges, especially where the peaty soil remains moist, grows the **Alder Buckthorn** (*Frangula alnus* Miller). One of the heralds of spring is the bright yellow brimstone butterfly flitting through the broken sunlight. She lays her eggs on this tree. Scrape the black bark of the twigs and the inner bark beneath is bright yellow and it is this layer that is used for medicines. It contains a number of active compounds, which have had various names, in the group known as anthraquinone glycosides. These include the frangulins which release emodin and so the prepared, dried bark of Alder Buckthorn is a long-established treatment for constipation. It is milder and safer than some alternatives but not suitable for all cases of constipation. The emodins in the blood stream have a cathartic action, stimulating the nerves of the colon, causing it to tighten up and increase its rhythmic action. When constipation is due to a tense colon then obviously this is not the medicine to prescribe.

It would also be avoided if the patient is pregnant or has haemorrhoids. Take too much of the stuff and the system suffers irritation, causing vomiting, diarrhoea and a rise in temperature. Fortunately people are unlikely to chew the twigs to the extent of being poisoned and even cases of livestock poisoning are rare. Children might eat the berries though. These ripen from green, through reddish purple to black, and black is a traditional warning that these are for the devil only. Eat too many and the medicinal values are exceeded, not only causing stomach upsets but kidney damage, muscular convulsions and collapse.

Down in the boggy areas grows the tiny **Sundew** (*Drosera rotundifolia* L.). It is tiny enough to sit comfortably in a teaspoon yet is of great economic importance on the Continent, for their inclusion in herbal medicines for respiratory problems. It relaxes the breathing muscles. The British Pharmacopoeia has said (in the 1993 ed. for example) that it was of 'doubtful value' but science has progressed, spurred on in part by the search for anti-cancer compounds, and we now know that not only is it antispasmodic and antitussive for breathing problems but has also an anti-bacterial, action (effective against Streptococcus, Staphylococcus, and the Pneumococcus bacteria). Other anti-microbial and general antibiotic action is being investigated. These actions are thought to come, in part at least, from plumbagin, a polyphenol of the naphthaquinone group. That can have undesirable side affects such as stomach upsets, while handling the crushed leaves of Sundew can cause dermatitis. Nevertheless, used wisely, this can be valuable to medicine and there has been work on synthesising the naphthaquinones. However, the active chemistry of these insectivorous plants is complex and still being investigated. Farmers have considered it toxic for hundreds of years: in the 16th century John Gerard reported that in the north it was the cause of 'Red Rot' because '*it rotteth sheep that eat of it,*' while in Scotland it was believed to cause the cattle disease called Earnach. In recent times thinking moved to considering whether some of the diseases recorded in history may have derived from mineral deficiencies, where the livestock had been grazing the incredibly poor soils beloved of the Sundew. While it was cursed on one hand it was exploited on the other – it has been important in alchemy, brewing and for curdling milk for cheese making. Now, ironically, it is proving effective in removing toxins from contaminated soil. It's an amazing little plant and no doubt current research will yield more wonders and values.

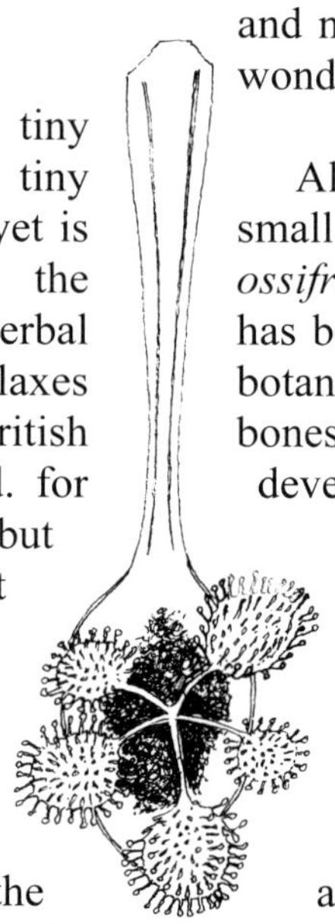

Also to be found in the boggy areas is the small but beautiful **Bog Asphodel** (*Narthecium ossifragum* L.). Just like the Sundew, this plant has been blamed for diseases in livestock. Its botanical name, *ossifragum*, means 'fragile bones'. This reflects a sad condition that can develop in lambs grazing the heathlands and was blamed upon this plant. Modern understanding is that it results from calcium deficiency on these acid soils, rather than any toxicity in the plant. However, Bog Asphodel is poisonous. Ingestion produces compounds that cause liver damage, leading to the animal becoming sensitive to light, resulting in sunburn and deterioration of the tissues. It affects the unpigmented skin of white lambs, rather than black lambs, and causes considerable economic loss in Norway where the disease is known as 'alveld'. The wild moose in southern Norway develop severe kidney disease too as do cattle across the Northern European areas with acid peat bog grazing lands. It is not known for certain which compounds are responsible.

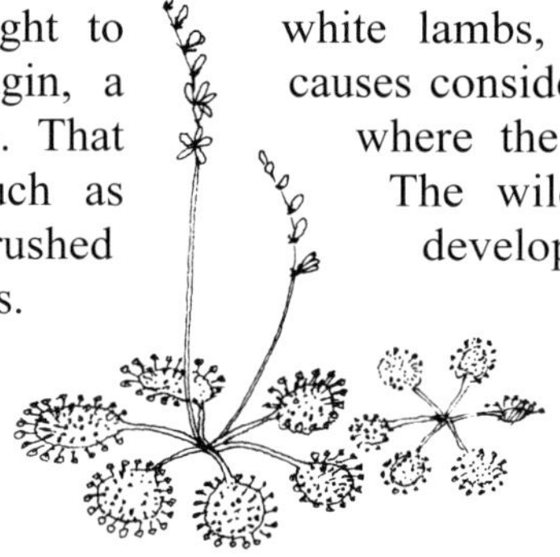

For many years the cause was thought to be the saponins (specifically the sapogenins known as sarsasapogenin and smilagenin) but tests have disproved this as being the sole cause (when lambs were fed on the plant they did not develop alveld). Attention turned to the likely mineral deficiencies in the soil of the grazing lands. Plots were treated with top-dressings of calcium and phosphorus to check whether these were involved. The phosphorus killed off the Bog Asphodel after three years but the plant was tolerant of calcium. Neither mineral affected the saponins content in the plant and lambs on the site still developed alveld. The disease persisted wherever the Bog Asphodel remained until the fifth year and then it stopped. They've looked at the different types of blood in the lambs and shown different levels of susceptibility between the two types of haemoglobin but that was still not the whole answer. They have started taking a broader view in the search for clues, and are interested now in a fungus, *Pithomyces chartarum,* that causes photosensitisation in the livestock of some countries, and are looking for it in Norway. Meanwhile, the beautiful little Bog Asphodel, is still viewed with suspicion. Much of the work is being done in Norway because alveld disease is of such economic importance there. It has implications in Britain, especially where sheep (and goats) are now being used for the sustainable heathland conservation.

**Bogbean** (*Menyanthes trifoliata* L.) is one of the most powerful medicinal plants in Britain, which has served us well for hundreds of years and still does so, as it proves of value for today's problems ranging from anti-cancer treatment to anorexia. It does have to be used with care and wisdom, however, for if consumed in excess it can have drastic action, described here by J. H. Millspaugh in 1892:-

"*Large doses of the root of this plant cause profuse vomiting and purging, together with exhausting diaphoresis [sweating]. Smaller doses cause confusion and vertigo, pressive headaches, dimness of vision, contraction of the pupil, twitching of the facial muscles, a sensation of coldness in the stomach and oesophagus, followed by nausea, distension and fullness of the abdomen, with griping, constipation, frequent desire to urine with scanty discharge, oppression of the chest with increased respiration and accelerated pulse, cramps in the legs, sleeplessness, coldness of the extremities, followed by fever without thirst, and extreme weakness of the whole body.*"

Heed the above. Despite these effects the plant gets classified rarely as poisonous. Indeed the Internet will yield dozens of pages that extol its virtues but few have any words of caution at all.

(Illus. courtesy of Janet Blight)

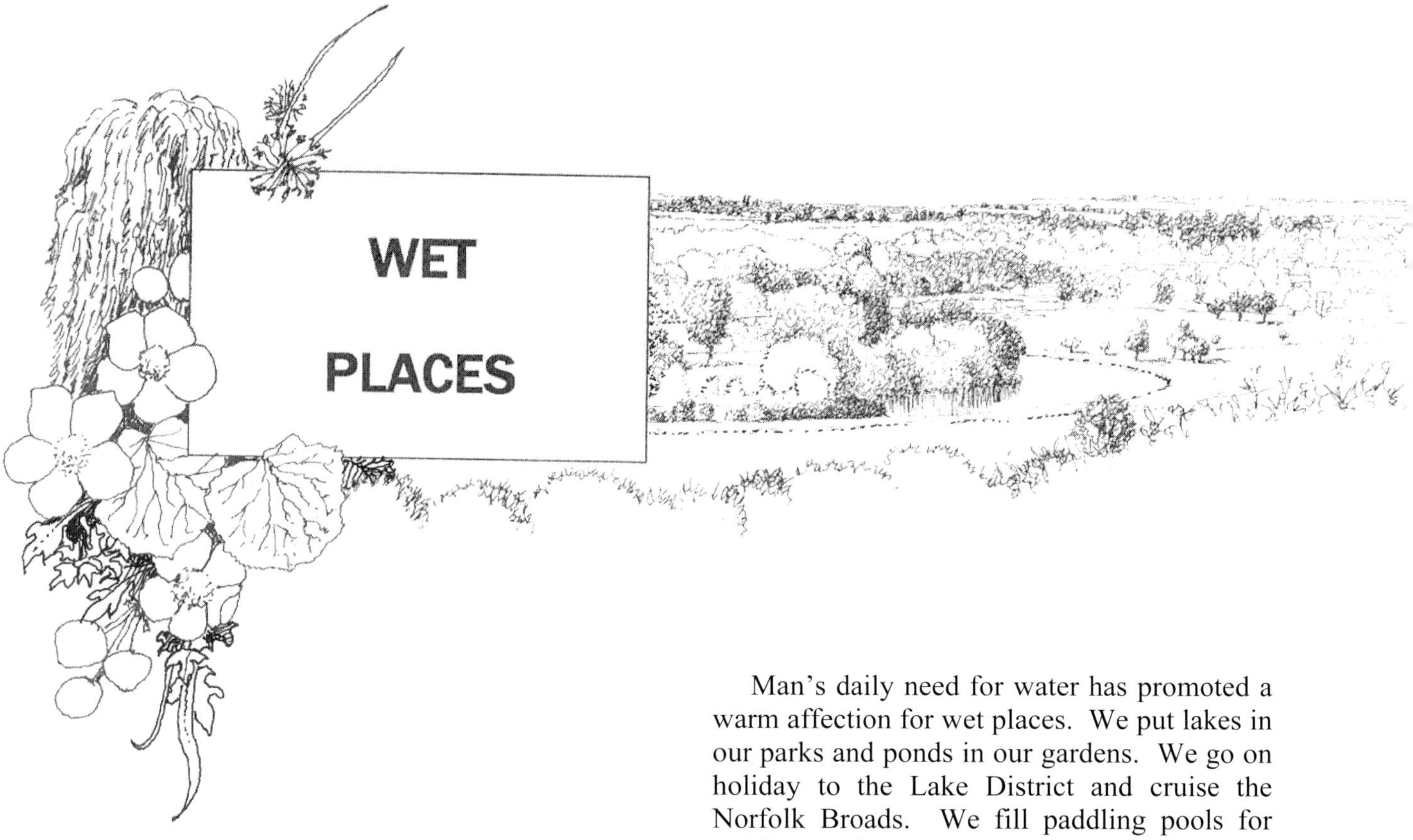

# WET PLACES

Man's daily need for water has promoted a warm affection for wet places. We put lakes in our parks and ponds in our gardens. We go on holiday to the Lake District and cruise the Norfolk Broads. We fill paddling pools for toddlers and engineer a babbling of running water outside our windows. We walk the river banks and fish from gaps among the reeds. Those reeds and other marginals grow thick and lush. They have always attracted herds of herbivores so surely these are places where plants must defend themselves vigorously. Surprisingly few do so. Instead of toxins, most rely on out-growing the grazers. There are some exceptions of course. Many of the buttercup family like moist places and here too grows one of Britain's most lethal plants, the Hemlock Water Dropwort.

First up in the spring is the **Marsh Marigold** (*Caltha palustris* L) and how luscious and tempting it looks too. Into the cooking pot this used to go by the handful – lovely fresh greens again. It was a mixed blessing. Yes, it's rich in much-needed vitamin C but on the other hand, this is a member of the buttercup family. It therefore contains toxins of the protoanemonine group. Back in 1862 C. P. Johnson cited from a Dr.Christison the case of "*five persons, who from poverty were compelled to resort to wild herbs for food, were poisoned by eating the Marsh Marigold. They were all seized with violent sickness and pain in the abdomen, followed by diarrhoea and general oedematous swelling over the whole body, but eventually recovered.*" Presumably they ate it fresh. It's much safer after cooking and indeed has been promoted regularly for steaming as spring greens, in Europe and North America. The Native American Abnaki, Alaska, Chippewa, Eskimo, Menominee, Mohegan and Objibwa nations all used it – but were careful to cook it first. It is a bit challenging to cook it long enough to render it safe and yet not so long as to destroy its nutritive value. Another popular option was to pickle the flower buds as a substitute for capers but Anne Pratt cites a Professor Burnett asserting that the vinegar would actually increase the toxic action. Using the plant medicinally has not proven very rewarding. Inevitably, with its bright gold flowers, it has been tried for yellow jaundice, as per the Doctrine of Signatures, believing that God gave it yellow flowers as a sign of his intended purpose. Trying to burn off warts with the caustic juice was not very successful either but people tried anything, in desperation, because warts were deemed to be a sign of the Devil. Toothache could be treated with it, said William Turner in the 17th century, but by the 19th century, C. P. Johnson etc. were pointing out that it would blister and burn the mouth. It is best left to simply enjoy as a brazen herald of spring and to that end it was one of the 'Mays' used to celebrate May Day.

Other species of *Rannunculus* enjoy wet places too, so look out for the yellow **Spearworts** and the white **Water Crowfoots**. The latter grow in the water itself, making restless green pillows in the currents of the chalk streams, embroidered over in early summer with big white buttercups. All are toxic but there is none more so than the **Celery-leaved Buttercup** (*Ranunculus sceleratus* L) with puny little yellow flowers on luscious foliage. The growth attracts grazing cattle, especially as it likes to grow in the poached mud around their watering places, and so they can consume it in large amounts – with lethal results. Thus it is regarded as the most toxic of the whole genus but this may be due to the cattle eating larger amounts.

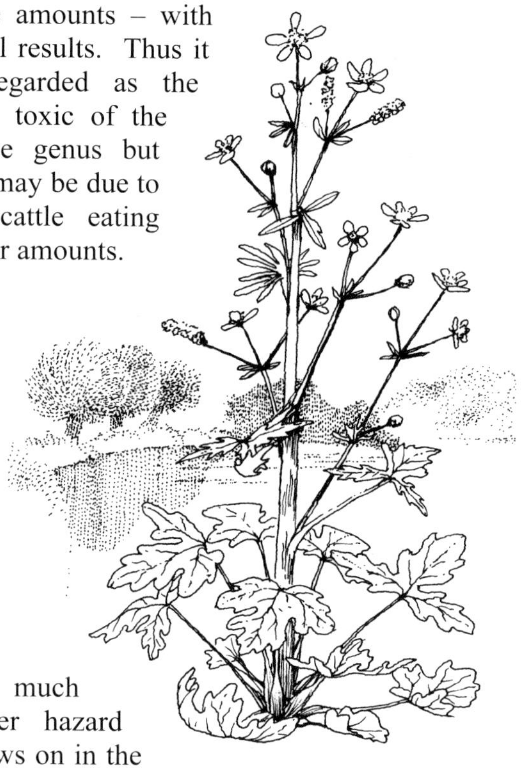

A much greater hazard follows on in the year from the Marsh Marigolds and that goes under the clumsy great name of **Hemlock Water Dropwort** (*Oenanthe crocata* L) which is not to be confused with its famous relative, the true Hemlock (*Conium maculatum* L). Far more telling are some of its regional names like Dead Man's Fingers and Dead Man's Oatmeal, for this is a plant that has caused a whole string of lurid human fatalities. It is one of the wild parsley family with umbrella heads of white blooms, that people find so confusing. This one is easy to recognise because it is the only one with stems deeply grooved like celery – so much so that when the new growth to shoot in the spring it has been mistaken for wild celery and for some people that has been a fatal mistake. Wild Celery does not really look like supermarket celery and it tastes very bitter. The *Oenanthe* is a particular hazard today since the media have been busy promoting natural foods. This plant should be nobody's food. How beautiful it is though, when in early summer it hummocks up great mounds of much-divided leaves overtopped with the white umbels. It seems to be increasing in many districts and can be found readily enough wherever there is moisture, from river and canal banks to wet fields and city culverts. Man has gathered the leaves for salads, the stems as celery and the tuberous roots for slicing and eating raw or adding to the cooking pot. They have been mistaken for turnips and parsnips. When labourers have been ditching they have unearthed the tuberous roots and left them in the spoil on the bank-side where livestock have eaten them, often fatally. All manner of livestock have been affected – horses and cattle, pigs and sheep. The French call it *Mort aux vache* and *Herbes sardonique* while the Americans call it Cursed Crowfoot. No doubt losses became more prevalent once livestock became familiar with eating root crops, after turnips had been introduced into British agriculture as a winter feed, from the mid 17th century onwards. In famine years man has tried them too. Drying the roots does not reduce their toxicity (remember Dead Man's Oatmeal !) and neither does drying it in hay render it safe. The toxicity is due to polyacetylenes, principally oenanthetoxin, which is the cis-isomer of cicutoxin. This takes its name from *Cicuta virosa*, **Cowbane**, which is another dangerous relative of the Hemlock Water Dropwort but not commonly found, fortunately. Bane, as in Cowbane, is an old Saxon word for a murderer or something that destroys life, especially a poison. This one is virulent, belonging to a

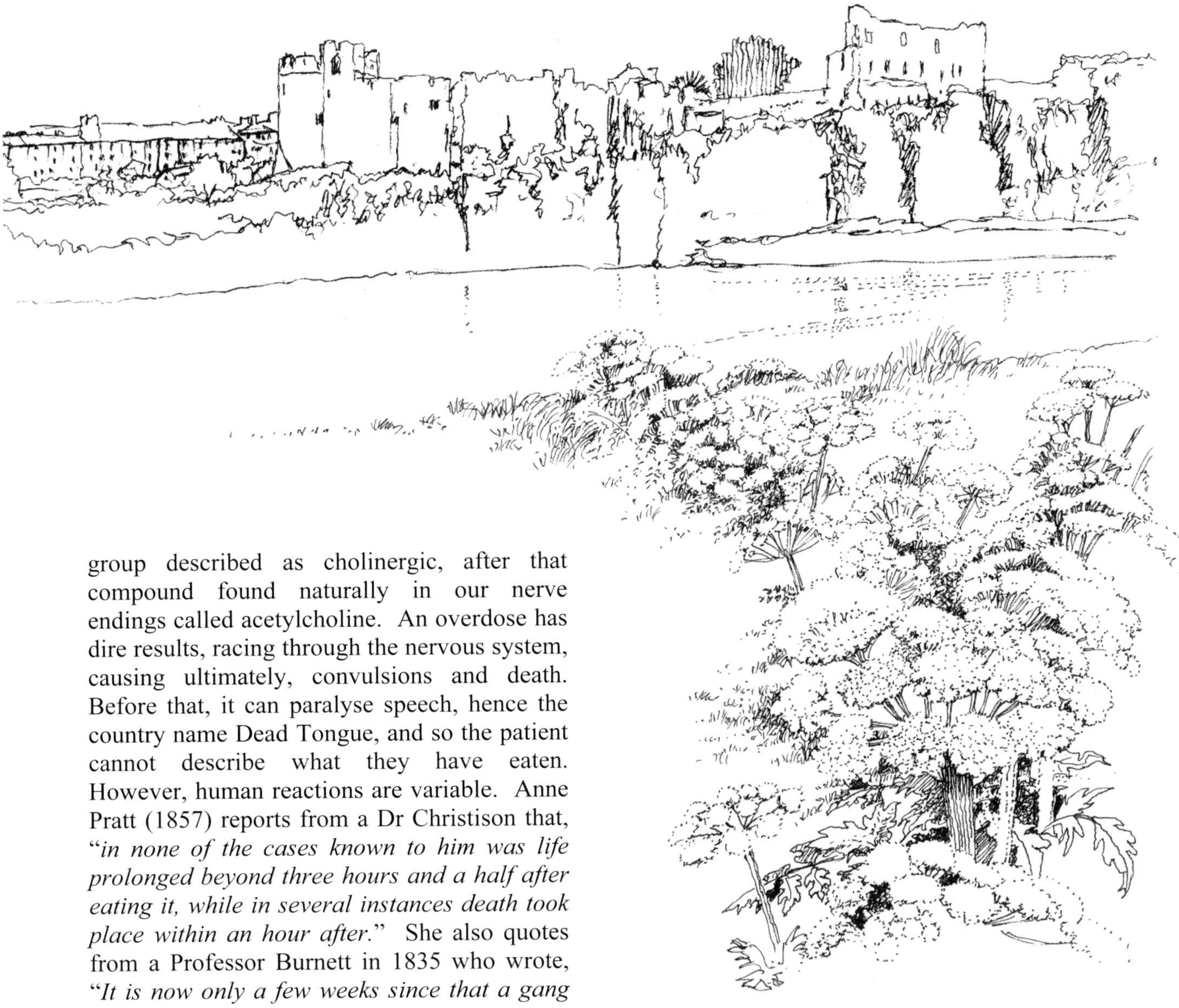

group described as cholinergic, after that compound found naturally in our nerve endings called acetylcholine. An overdose has dire results, racing through the nervous system, causing ultimately, convulsions and death. Before that, it can paralyse speech, hence the country name Dead Tongue, and so the patient cannot describe what they have eaten. However, human reactions are variable. Anne Pratt (1857) reports from a Dr Christison that, "*in none of the cases known to him was life prolonged beyond three hours and a half after eating it, while in several instances death took place within an hour after.*" She also quotes from a Professor Burnett in 1835 who wrote, "*It is now only a few weeks since that a gang of convicts, working on the embankments at Woolwich, dug up a considerable quantity of the roots of this Dropwort; and as they are fleshy, and have a not unpleasant smell and taste, seventeen of the unfortunate men ate them. They were all more or less disordered, some extremely ill, and four died from the effects of poison.*" Back in 1698 there were concerns over this plant, with a letter to the Royal Society from John Ray, quoted by Richard Mabey in *Flora Britannica* passing on a report from Dr Francis Vaughan that in Tipperary eight boys had eaten this plant on a fishing trip and, "*About four or Five Hours after going home, the Eldest of them...on a sudden fell down backwards, and lay kicking and sprawling on the Ground, his Countenance soon turned very Ghastly, and he foamed at the Mouth. Soon after Four more were seized the same way, and they all died before Morning, not one of them having spoken a word....Of the other Three One ran stark Mad, but came to his right Reason again the next Morning. Another had his hair and nails faln off...*" Both Anne Pratt and Richard Mabey draw our attention to a report by John Lightfoot (1777) that carries an important warning to anyone tempted to gather this plant as a cut-flower. The botanical artist Georg Ehret brought some indoors to draw but "*the smell, or effluvia only, rendered him so giddy that he was several times obliged to quit the room, and walk out in the fresh air to recover himself; but recollecting at last what might probably be the cause of his repeated illness, he opened the door and windows of the room, and the free air then enabled him to finish his work without any more return of his giddiness.*"

Bright gold flags of the **Wild Iris** (*Iris* pseudacorus L) are the next to come into bloom. They have long been suspected of causing poisoning in cattle and subsequently a glycoside was isolated from Irises that was named iridin (or irisin/irisine). It is found throughout the plant but especially in the rhizomes, so gardeners need to be wary of getting Iris juice on their skin when dividing up the garden clumps. It makes the skin sensitive to light with most unpleasant results. Similarly, conservation workers grubbing out overgrown clumps from the village pond need to be wary. If the compound is ingested it has a purgative action, causing vomiting and diarrhoea, but a larger dose results in fever and possible death. Used wisely it can stimulate the liver and act as a blood cleanser, but on the whole it has been used little in herbal medicines. Instead the Wild Iris has been used as a source of dyes and fibre and most recently, as a natural sewage purifier.

Pure water is needed for Watercress and so it grows best along the chalk streams but there is another look-alike plant that is far less fussy and that is **Fool's Watercress** (*Apium nodiflorum* (L) Lag.) which seems to be going through a name change to **Marshwort**. This is a dubious entry in this book, for although it is recognised as poisonous in some countries, such as the United States, it does not seem to have caused harm in Britain. Indeed it is said to have been chopped and added to the original Cornish pasties and is known in Devon as Pie Cress. However, it may not be wise to try it since it could be contaminated with pollutants out of the water. Even the genuine Watercress, if gathered from the wild, can result in us having nasty parasitic worms, so both are best left alone.

**Rushes** (*Juncus* spp.) are also suspect. They contain cyanide compounds and therefore ought to be toxic but cattle have grazed water-meadows for centuries without these plants becoming a major hazard. Observation reveals that rushes are not palatable and the livestock graze round them, except sometimes when the rushes are very young. Presumably it is only when all other fodder has been grazed that livestock are forced to graze them in quantity. Logically rushes ought to have been even commoner in the days before modern drainage but on the other hand, if they were cut regularly for strewing on floors their seed production would have been curtailed. The church had its rush-bearing Sundays before seed dispersal, usually near 29th June, St. Peter's Day (he was patron of the open fields), but in general practice rush-gathering was often delayed until September. Even the churches could not always get enough rushes and so swept half to the back to serve another year.

# AT HOME

Home should be safe. It's where we relax and rarely think about the poisonous plants around us, certainly not on the dinner plate. This relaxed attitude can make our homes the most dangerous of places. That has become particularly true during the last thirty years when we have turned increasingly to prepared and processed foods from the supermarkets. Consequently children have grown up unable to recognise the raw materials of food and certainly not able to name them. Indeed we have reached the stage where thousands of children refuse to eat fresh fruit and veg. That is all changing at the time of writing, with a movement to return us to fresh produce. Children's eating habits are a particular concern, with much effort towards improvement, whether at home or at school. There is a new generation of children growing up with a liking for green leaves and coloured berries. Yipes! Are toddlers going to start nibbling leaves and berries in the garden, especially as so many people are turning to home-grown produce again? It's time for those with knowledge to share it with the younger generations. Our local shop had potatoes in the window, where they had turned green, and the shop manager, in his twenties, thought my polite requests to dump them and change his practice were absolutely absurd. It took action from the Environmental Health Authorities to convince him. The next year we had green spuds back in the window. The manager had changed and the story starts again. Older readers will know the dangers of green potatoes. Younger people don't. Even the most urbanised people come into direct contact with poisonous plants. They are part of daily life.

This last chapter highlights some of the plants that create hazards around our homes. The original idea was to concentrate upon native plants that are now rare in the wild but frequent in gardens – Daphne and Daffodils and Lily of the Valley – but that idea has been expanded to highlight some of the introduced species. This is only a selection though. Problems arise where species have been developed into a more desirable form as a garden cultivar and it is not known whether the genes for toxicity have passed through the breeding programme – celery and lettuce are two examples that have gone through great changes. Where gardens are frequented by young children and pets it would be wise to check for toxicity. This is particularly important for 'new' introductions by the horticulture industry since these have not had chance to build up reputations with gardeners. These new introductions can be particularly difficult if they are marketed without bearing the Latin name of the species from which they were developed. Some plant families are more likely to have poisonous members than others – the Solanaceae, Rannunculaceae and Leguminoseae for example – and this should alert purchasers to check toxicity. The most dangerous of the currently fashionable plants include **Angels' Trumpets** (*Brugmansia*), **Monkshood** (*Aconitum*) and **Castor Oil Plant** (*Ricinus*). The plea for Garden Centres to label poisonous plants as such is a simple idea but an impossibility. Yes, some plants will poison people at the nibble of a leaf while others require the consumption of large amounts, beyond what might be expected as 'normal' behaviour from us. Other plants are more likely to affect out pets, as can happen when cats lick Lily pollen off their fur or the wind blows toxic seeds into an outdoor aviary or the mower/strimmer strews clippings into the fish pond.

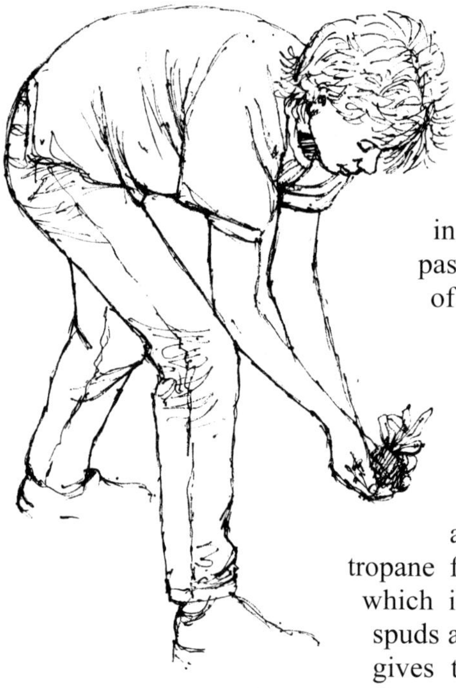

We would imagine that anything sold as food would be perfectly safe; after all, we're always being told that Britain has the strictest legislation in the world for food safety. That does indeed safeguard us to a high degree. It's what we do with the food that can be hazardous – like leaving potatoes to go green. They are the most toxic plant in our everyday lives. We are told that tea and coffee would not pass our strict safety regulations nowadays but are permitted out of established practice. The same applies to Potatoes.

**Potatoes** (*Solanum tuberosum* L.) belong to the Solanaceae family, which is one of only three families in the world that contain tropane toxins. These affect the brain and are the most lethal of all. The tropane found in Potatoes is called solanin, which is present at all times, whether the spuds are green or not. It's the solanin that gives the potato most of its flavour, so when we enthuse that the potatoes are tasty this week, we are enjoying an enrichment of the poison. It amounts to about 90 parts per million although that varies, along with the flavour. Such a concentration equals about a quarter of the lethal dose for a human. Fear not, we would have to eat something like 14-20lb in a meal to get killed ! However, the situation changes dramatically if the tubers are exposed to light and thereby stimulated into growth. First they start producing chlorophyll – the green stuff, and alongside that solanin develops for chemical protection. The longer the tubers are exposed to light the deeper the chlorophyll/solanin develops. Even lightly greened potato is highly toxic. Cut it all off thoroughly before cooking.

Even in the dark, potatoes will start to sprout and these new growing points are protected heavily with solanin and must be removed. At the same time cut out the area around the base – the 'eye' -from which it grew. Any large eyes that have not yet started to sprout should be removed too. They are developing concentrations of solanin ready for growth. Do not take chances in the hope that the solanin will be destroyed in the cooking, since heat does not destroy it. Treated wisely, potatoes are a nutritive and important part of our diets.

We have had them since the 16th century, when they were introduced to Europe from the New World. The wild Solanums of potato type are upland plants, from the South American Andes, through the Mexican Sierra Madre and into the United States up as far as Wyoming. There may be 200 or more species but domestication has confused the picture, with several thousand different cultivars; the peoples of each high mountain valley have developed their own cultivar in isolation. Some of these early genetic strains are now important for yielding the genes for making solanin etc. that in turn makes the plant disease resistant. Now that the potato has become such an important world food it is vital we maintain its natural resistance to disease rather than try to breed out the solanin. We don't want another disaster like the blight that spread across Europe in the early 19th century, culminating in the infamous Irish Potato Famine, when well over a million Irish died and another million emigrated. By displacing so many Irish families the humble potato changed world history, especially in the United States where they now have several million American-Irish families.

From the same family comes the **Tomato** (*Lycopersicon esculentum* Miller). It too originated in South America, and was first seen by Europeans in 1520 when Spanish conquistadors, led by Hernando Cortez, spotted some in an Aztec market. The tomatoes were cherry-sized and called *tomatl* or *xtomatl* – putting an Aztec word into our vocabulary. Seed was sent home to Spain in 1522 and from there to Italy (under Spanish rule) to be grown first at Naples in 1523. That's the usual story, based upon Dodoens' book, *Historie of Plants*, published in 1578. Having Spanish and therefore Roman Catholic associations, worked against Tomatoes. So did the fact that Jewish people in Britain were more adventurous with them since many Jews were of Spanish (and Portuguese) descent. Not only that, but putting Tomatoes into the nightshade family, frightened the British into fearing they were deadly poisonous. The adventurous-timid cooked them, for hours, to render them safe.

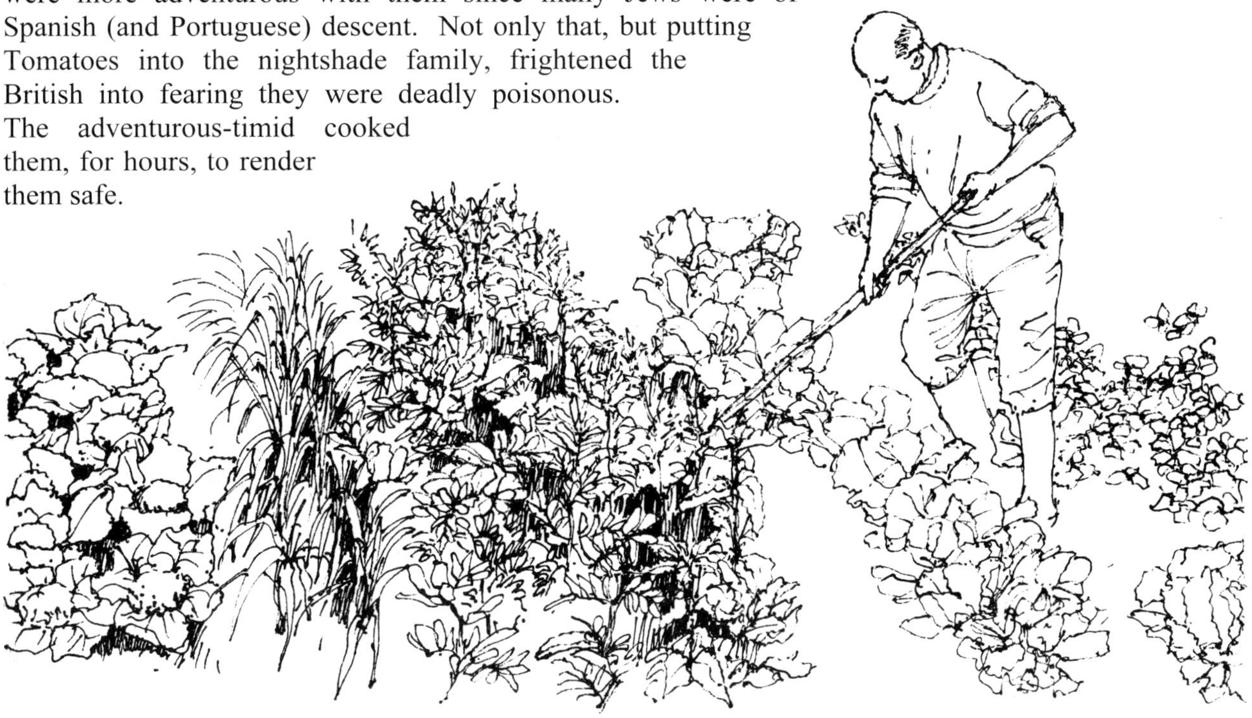

Thus these fruits became a 'vegetable' but not much notice was taken of them. For a long time there was only a narrow range of cultivars available, descended from the wild species. Even in the 1930s people were still afraid of them and were likely to cook them for hours in casseroles etc. Then in the 1940s a selective plant breeding programme led to the first F1 hybrid tomato coming on the market – bred by Dr. Oved Shifriss and introduced by W. Atlee, as 'Big Boy'. That was only in 1949. Since then, hundreds of cultivars have been introduced, making it a crop of enormous economic value, especially as its nutritive value has become more generally acknowledged and the finding of a powerful anti-cancer compound in Tomatoes has enhanced their reputation further.

While the plant is busy growing it defends itself against attack with more of those powerful tropanes that interfere with the transmission of impulses from nerve cell to nerve cell. They develop in the plant alongside the green chlorophyll, so it is the greenery and unripe fruits that are most toxic. One of the prime compounds is solanidine but as the fruit develops so the plant changes it to a milder compound called solanine. Other related compounds include chaconine, tomatine and tomatidine. Fortunately these compounds are not absorbed very well through the gut wall of mammals and even then the digestive system hydrolizes them into metabolites that are much safer. They are liable to be excreted rapidly too. Fortunately, a lot of the toxic material has to be absorbed before symptoms of poisoning occur, and the more poisonous green tomatoes are normally used for chutney that is not consumed in large amounts. In contrast, Tomatoes contain other powerful compounds that are of enormous benefit to us, such as lycopene. That reduces the risk of certain cancers, especially prostate cancer, but also lung, bladder, cervix, skin and digestive tract cancers. It is also good at warding off heart disease and stopping the arteries from clogging up. It does this by preventing the oxidation of low density lipoproteins (LDLs). So the general message is to eat tomatoes regularly. Opinions differ as to how many and how often but four large tomatoes a day is a popular suggestion. Even one large tomato a day will be beneficial in warding off the bone deterioration disease, osteoporosis. To boost our daily intake we can include processed products, such as tomato sauce and soup, because the processing renders the lycopene easier to absorb.

For those who grow their own vegetables there is a hazard with the leaves of **Rhubarb** (*Rheum x hybridum* gp). Modern Rhubarb is a hybrid derived from interbreeding a few of the twenty or so species of Rheum in the world. The original Garden Rhubarb was *Rheum Rhaponticum*, which originates from Siberia but was grown widely before being introduced into Britain in 1573. That was cross-bred with *R. officinale*, which originates from Tibet and was introduced in 1871, but that too was grown widely for its medicinal values. Rhubarb was a medicine (an effective laxative) long before it was a food. The Chinese have used it medicinally for over 2,000 years. It was not until the early 1800s that the stems started to be cooked and served as a substitute for fruit. At the same time there were warnings about its potential toxicity. It is of course very acid, and so for decades cooks have been boiling Rhubarb in tarnished cooking pots in order to clean them. Anything that scours metal pots and pans so effectively might well be injurious to our innards. Never consume Rhubarb stems that have been cooked in a copper vessel nor consume the leaves.

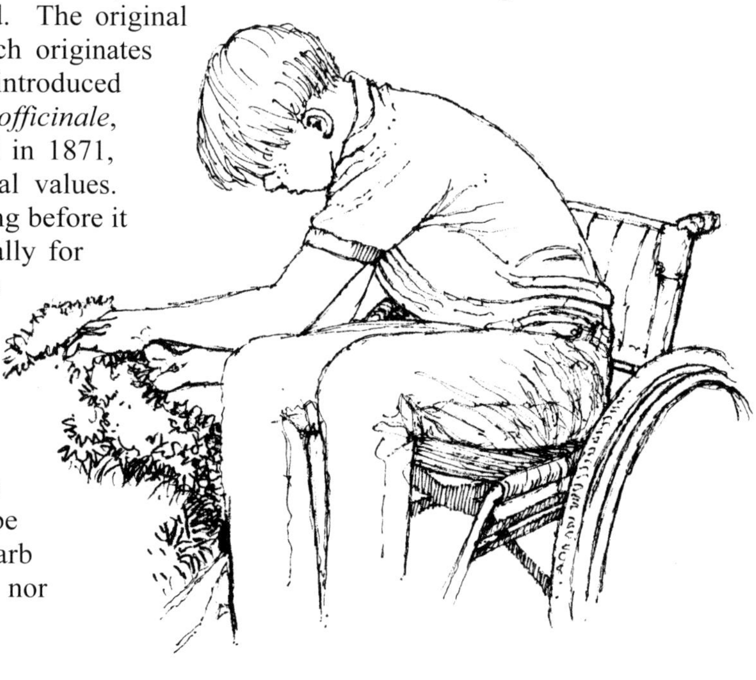

Fatalities from eating the leaves, cooked like cabbage, were being reported soon after the mid 19th century. They contain oxalic acid – oxalates of calcium and potassium, which produce the symptoms of poisoning, with pain, nausea and muscle spasms, before the liver and kidneys are affected. This may not be the whole picture. There is concern that the poisoning may result, in part at least, from anthraquinone glycosides.

In the same family as Rhubarb are the Sorrels, used as salad flavouring and available widely from Garden Centres and herb specialists. Usually this is the **French Sorrel** (*Rumex scutatus* L.) rather than our native **Common Sorrel** (*Rumex acetosa* L) but they are still of the genus *Rumex* along with the toxic Docks. It is thought that people have a greater tolerance of the oxalates in Sorrel than in Docks, especially the French Sorrel, but even so, use them sparingly and at intervals, otherwise they too can cause stomach pains and cramps, nausea and vomiting, and diarrhoea. They can also lower the level of calcium in the blood, causing muscle spasms and can lead eventually to kidney and liver problems. Some people get an allergic reaction to Sorrel, such as breathing difficulties or skin irritation.

These oxalates recur when we look at **Spinach** (*Spinacea oleracea* L.) but the dangers of over-eating this are better publicised and those who enjoy it are more likely to know that it should not be eaten more often than about twice a week. That allows our bodies to deal with the oxalates. This is one of the 'wonder' vegetables for all the vitamins and minerals it contains and the health enhancing actions it promotes, helping ward off such diverse problems as anaemia, birth defects, cancer, degenerative eye disease, heart disease and stroke. Even so, the oxalates make it an unwise choice for people with kidney and bladder stones or gout. Always eat it straight after cooking else it can become toxic in different ways and do avoid re-heating it. Fresh young leaves are the most valuable of all; better to have them from frozen than to eat fresh *old* leaves. Canned Spinach contains most of the virtues of the fresh with the notable exception of folic acid. Raw Spinach is becoming popular and justly so. It promotes haemoglobin in the red blood cells, which carries oxygen, and so more oxygenated blood gets to our brains and muscles etc. It also helps balance the pH levels in the blood and so avoid other problems. Indeed it even reduces toxicity in the soil – it's being cropped on soils contaminated with lead so that the plants absorb the metal. Then the contaminated plants can be removed. Spinach is the 'Prince of vegetables' in the Islamic world and it was the Moslems who took it to Spain from where it spread to western Europe in the 11th century. It didn't become popular until the 16th century onwards and today, as we understand more of its values, it's becoming a major European crop.

News headlines in recent years have made people much more aware that dried beans can be highly poisonous. This refers to the dried seeds of the **Red Kidney Bean** (*Phaseolus coccineus* L.) used in Chilli Con Carne but can apply just as importantly to **Runner Beans** (*Phaseolus vulgaris* L.), (the mature seeds rather than sliced green beans), which some people have tried as a substitute. It is the slow gentle cooking, as in casseroles, that is so dangerous because the temperature does not rise high enough to destroy the toxins. If undercooked or raw, the Red Kidney Beans have between 100x and 175x more toxins than when cooked. White Beans have only a third as much and Broad Beans only 5-10% as much. For safe cooking, Kidney Beans should be soaked beforehand, for at least five hours, and then strained and rinsed. Boil them vigorously for at least ten minutes and then they are fit to add to recipes for the slow cooker etc. The toxic compounds are lectins, primarily phytohaemaglutin, which affects the lymphocytes, red blood cells, and cell function. They are valuable in medicine, especially in treatments for HIV, but it takes only four of five uncooked beans to cause symptoms of poisoning. That starts in 1-3 hours with vomiting, often severe, followed later by diarrhoea. Cases can be serious and result in hospitalisation. Comparing the number of reports of poisoning in Britain with other countries, such as the United States, it looks as though the British are particularly prone to undercook their beans, so take care.

Most other vegetables are safe in the quantities we would normally eat. There is concern over erucic acid, found in brassicas such as **Broccoli**, but again we are unlikely to eat enough to cause poisoning. All the brassicas contain glucosinolates which get broken down into isothiocyanates which protects us from cancers. Similarly, there are concerns over nitrate levels, where growers have saturated their land with these fertilisers to promote plenty of growth in their leaf vegetables. The plants absorb and store the nitrates. This can apply to produce that has been grown free of chemical fertilisers if large amounts of animal dung have been used instead. Currently the advice being published is to put as much variety into our diets as possible, on a daily basis, and to vary it from day to day, keeping served portions in moderation.

Turning to fruit, one of the chief dangers to look out for is amygdalin, which is a bitter compound, reminding us again that many toxins taste bitter, hence the development of special taste buds for bitterness on our tongues. Amygdalin occurs frequently in the seeds of members of the rose family, the Rosaceae, which includes fruits such as **Almonds, Apples, Apricots, Cherries, Peaches** and **Plums,** so it is very much part of our everyday lives. This compound is a cyanogenic glycoside, composed of mandelic nitrile and gentobiose. When consumed, our enzymes split these two components and then a second enzyme action converts the mandelic nitrile into benzaldehyde and hydrocyanic acid. The first gives us the bitter almonds taste while the second is the highly toxic substance. It is so toxic that about 20 bitter almonds are considered a lethal dose for an adult, but reported cases are rare. There are more for children, who will succumb to ten kernels or less. To eat Bitter Almonds at all is deemed "Very Dangerous." If the poisoning is slight the consumer may simply vomit. In serious cases the heart accelerates, the head goes dizzy and regular breathing breaks down. Death follows. This is definitely something to use in tiny doses for flavouring only. It is also used in perfumery. Such an active compound has been explored in medicine and in carefully controlled doses can relax the muscles, especially those of the digestive system, but there are much safer alternatives. The search for anti-cancer drugs has led to fresh

reviews of the compound and it has been claimed that a substance called laetrile, derived from the amygdalin, is indeed effective against some cancers. Countries like the United States disagreed and declared it was not effective. It is still highly controversial. Use remains limited, largely because the risk of cyanide poisoning is considered too high. In contrast, **Sweet Almonds** are safe because by the time they have ripened they have lost their amygdalin content – except for about 1% of the crop. Produce from some sources, such as California, is claimed to be totally free of amygdalin. **Apples** are safe unless the pips are eaten; children have died from eating too many Apple pips.

**Bulbs, Tubers and Corms**

These organs of food storage are obviously prone to attack by the hungry and should therefore have pronounced chemical defences. Indeed they have! So many we looked at have proven toxins that the safest thing is to advise that all should be treated as hazardous. Few have proven to be drop-dead dangerous, with the exception of *Colchicum*, but they will make you ill if consumed. Fortunately each is large enough to keep track of, if planting pots in the kitchen, so the chances of them straying into food are far slighter than say spilling a packet of seeds. Even so, do not leave them unattended if little children or pets might sample them. Workers in the horticulture industry are most at risk. Staff at Garden Centres report reactions, sometimes severe, when they open the bulk cartons of bulbs. Prolonged handling of Tulip and Hyacinth bulbs has proven especially dangerous but there are concerns that toxicity may be due, in part at least, to the fungicides and insecticides with which the consignment has been packed.

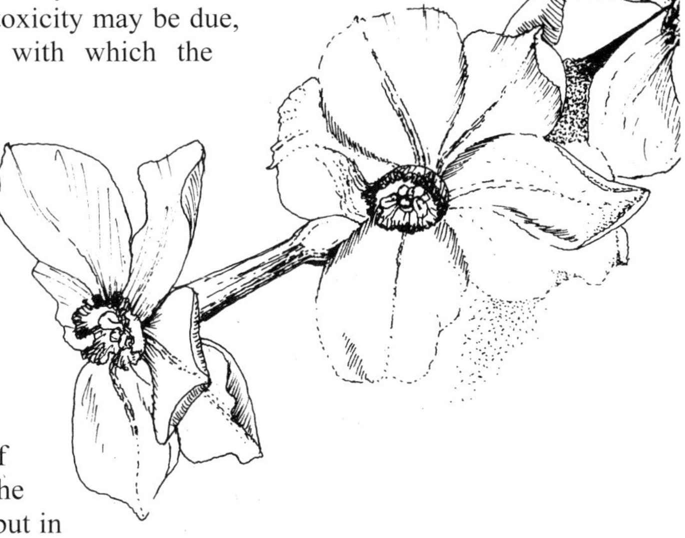

The commonest of these is the **Daffodil** (*Narcissus* spp. and hyb.) of which Britain grows more than any other nation. The name Narcissus derives from the same Greek as 'narcotic' and means 'numbness'. Pick bunches of Daffodils over a sustained period and the juice makes your hands go numb; in my childhood this was known as 'daffy dabs.' It takes quite some time to wear off. Consuming small amounts causes vomiting and so Daffodils have been used as an emetic for hundreds of years. Don't try it; it can be lethal. Large doses affect the central nervous system causing total paralysis and death but in controlled doses have been exploited for anaesthesia. Traditionally, Daffodils have been used in folk medicine for thousands of years, for a wide range of treatments since there are a number of active compounds. A prime one was isolated and given the name narcissine. Another was called lycorine but in 1920 they were proven to be the same alkaloid and the name lycorine has prevailed since. Among its modern medical applications is a treatment for malaria. The bulbs also contain an alkaloid called galanthamine or galantamine, after *Galanthus*, the **Snowdrop**. It is the affect that galanthamine has on the nervous system that has led it to an important treatment for Alzheimer's Disease and similar dementias. There has also been research in relation to epilepsy, palsy and chronic fatigue syndrome. Supplies of Snowdrop bulbs as a source of galanthamine soon proved inadequate and made the medicines extremely expensive, so Daffodil bulbs are now used as an additional source. To that end, fields of them are grown in Britain and Ireland for the pharmaceutical industry. Those in Wales are at an elevation of over 300m and it has been found that growing them at high altitudes increases their content of the valuable compounds. As we learn more about the Daffodil so we also verify some of the ancient treatments – the discovery of anti-fungal peptides in the plant explains its old use for treating discoloured skin. It is not a plant for home-made treatments though. Take care if you are potting bulbs in the kitchen. People have died from getting them mixed in with onions; the toxins are not destroyed by cooking. The late flowering Narcissus with white perianth and little orange cup, known as Pheasant's Eye etc. is thought to be the most toxic of all.

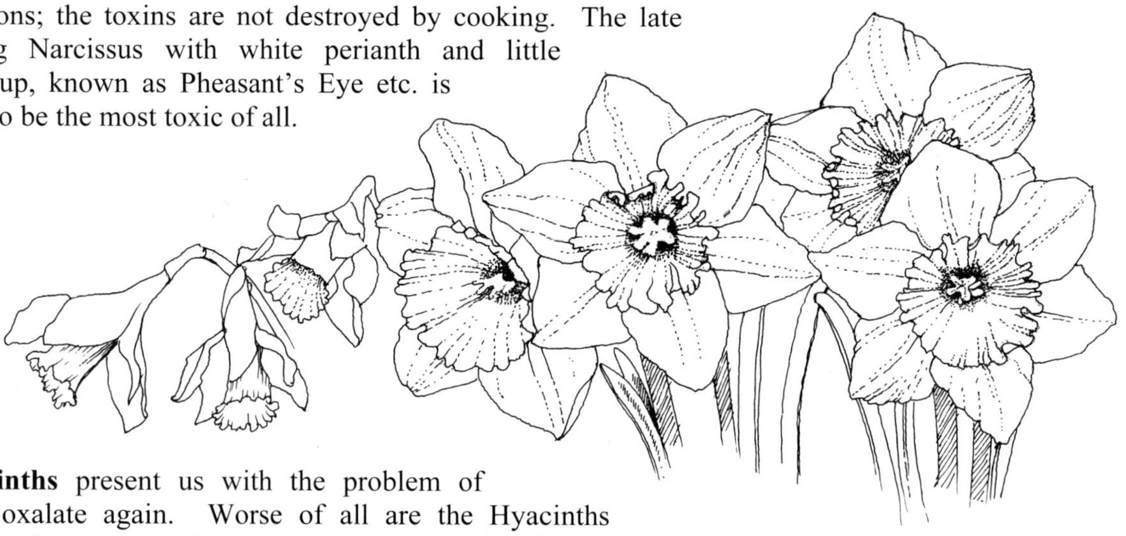

**Hyacinths** present us with the problem of calcium oxalate again. Worse of all are the Hyacinths themselves because they have papery scales round their bulbs which trap loose crystals and for this reason many Garden Centres now provide gloves for customers choosing their loose bulbs. Whether the dermatitis is caused exclusively by the calcium oxalate is not known for certain but seems to be doubted. Fungicides and pesticides are being reviewed, since some workers at garden centres suffer a reaction as soon as they open the big cartons of bulbs, which contain these chemicals treatments. What does seem clear is that Hyacinths are considered the most hazardous in this group and the Roman Hyacinth to be worst of all. Other members of the group may well have the needle-like crystals on the bulb surface from where they can rub into the skin and cause an irritant reaction. They also dust onto the work surface so beware if you are potting bulbs in the kitchen, and they penetrate clothing to give reactions in unexpected places. The little bulbs of spring, such as *Chionodox, Scilla* and *Muscari*, do not seem to have rung alarm bells particularly loudly. Avoid eating them as most are mildly toxic and do not handle excessively with bare hands. Otherwise, enjoy these uplifting heralds of spring.

Through spring and into early summer we can enjoy the **Fritillaries** (*Fritillaria*), from our dainty native **Snake's-head Lily** to the **Crown Imperial.** The latter comes from the Western Himalayas and was a very early introduction (before 1590) and on travels in that part of the world you might get the bulbs served up for food, especially in China. They seem to find it safe, when cooked, but the raw bulbs certainly are not. When tested, the glycosides (verticine, verticinone, imperialine and thymidine, etc.) produced effects such as dilated pupils, tremor, lowered blood pressure, decreased heart rate, declining respiration and secretions from glands were switched off. That sounds like atropine from Deadly Nightshade and indeed *Fritillaria* compounds have been used as an alternative, since they are some 20-30 times milder. They have a very long history in Eastern folk medicine but this should not lead us to try some ourselves since an overdose can be serious. It should be used only under professional guidance, and not by anybody who is pregnant.

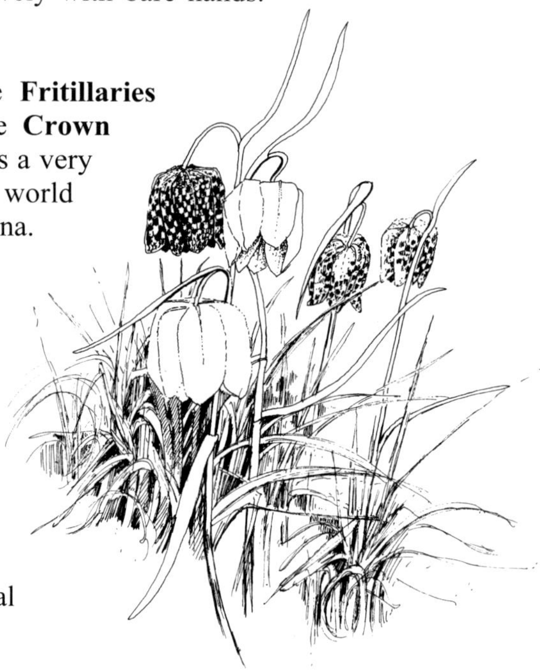

**Tulips** are foreign but have been in our gardens for hundreds of years and the yellow *Tulipa sylvestris* has even naturalised into the wild, although it is decreasing nowadays. Lots of people seem to know that during the privations of World War II the Dutch had to resort to eating their tulip bulbs, which resulted in fatalities, so it was a bit astonishing to find on the Internet a site that declared "*Tulip bulbs and petals are non-toxic.*" Oh no they are not. It then says, "*In fact, the tulip is the only spring bulb which is edible,*" followed by some culinary suggestions Do not try it. The bulbs contain a number of active compounds including lectins, and compounds known as tuliposide A and tuliposide B. The former changes into tulipalin A and is thought responsible for causing a sensitising reaction, which might have only a slight effect. Some people, however, get much more severe problems, with blistering, cracking and fissuring of their fingers, which can even lead to the loss of their finger tips. Workers in the bulb industry wear gloves when handling tulip bulbs but even then these must be made of synthetic rubber (Nitrile) since the toxins penetrate vinyl (polyvinyl chloride) gloves. Eating the bulbs enables the tulipan A to upset the digestive system, causing pain and vomiting. It leaves patients feeling weak and ill for days. It also affects the uptake of nutrients, so livestock are reported as dying weeks after they were fed the bulbs. It is the bulbs that have the greatest concentrations, then the leaves and least in the flowers. Plant breeders have been working to develop cultivars that are devoid of these toxins but for the moment it is safest to leave the turban blooms to feed our emotions and keep the bulbs out of the cooking pot.

The really dangerous bulb is autumn flowering – the **Autumn Crocus** (*Colchicum*) – and this includes the seeds too. We have exploited the powerful compounds in this plant, medicinally, for over 2,000 years. From Classical mythology we learn that the beautiful Medea had a secret garden of poisonous plants, among which she had a particular favourite with which to dispatch people. This was the story Linnaeus remembered when he classified the plants in the 18th century and named the genus after Medea's Mediterranean land of "Colchis." Plants of the genus contain colchicine, which is a tricyclic alkaloid, first isolated in 1820 by two French chemists, P.S. Pelletier and J. Caventon. This compound affects the cells, causing polyploidia, so it is used by plant breeders to double the number of chromosomes. With this effect, it is crucial that pregnant women do not take medicines containing colchicine, otherwise the baby may have birth defects or develop them later.

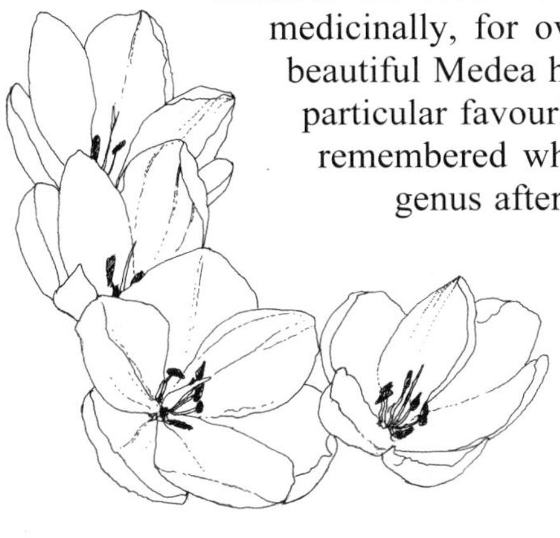

Similarly it is said men should avoid such medicines prior to fathering a child. Colchicine can also stop the cells dividing, and cause birth defects that way. Although we know what it does, researchers are not sure how it does it. Apart from cell damage, colchicines causes long-term damage to the kidneys and liver, nerves and muscles and the marrow. An overdose can be lethal in a few hours from multiple and painful affects around the body, leading to cardiac and respiratory failure. As little as 200mg has proved fatal. There is no antidote to the toxin itself but fortunately Colchicum poisoning is rare. Medicines containing colchicine are likely to be for one problem only – gout. The compound suppresses the inflammation, and thereby reduces the pain, and it also retards the frequency of attacks. There is another course of treatment, using this compound, and that's for Mediterranean Fever, a painful infection caught from handling livestock or drinking unpasteurised milk. It can be treated with antibiotics instead of colchicines. Indeed, colchicine is used rarely in medicines due to its high toxicity. Although, its cellular activity has been explored as a cancer treatment it has been rejected, since too high a dose would be needed.

**Garden Hedging, Trees and Shrubs**

Our traditional hedging plants are a poisonous lot. Hornbeam and Beech hedges are safe but Box, Holly, Laurel, Privet and Yew and conifers all carry hazards.

**Privet** of hedge fame occurs as two species in Britain. **Wild Privet** (*Ligustrum vulgare* L.) is a wild deciduous shrub of the southern counties, usually on alkaline soils. The near-evergreen hedging shrub is the **Oval-leaved Privet** (*Ligustrum ovalifolium* Hassk.), introduced from Japan in 1842. Both have white flowers in terminal panicles that develop into dull black berries. It is these that are believed to be more toxic than the foliage. The active compound is a glucoside referred to usually as ligustrin (oleonolic acid), which is an impure form of syringin (from members of the genus *Syringa*, Lilacs) or it is expressed as 'syringin ligustrin'. The action is irritation of the digestive system causing abdominal pain, vomiting and diarrhoea. It has killed children, cattle, horses and sheep. In countries such as New Zealand Privet must be removed from any property following a health complaint. With this in mind, children should be taught not to eat the berries while livestock should not be allowed to browse Privet hedges or be fed on hedge clippings. More cheerfully, the toxin has proved valuable in cancer treatment, especially in China and Japan. The Chinese discovered that regular doses had practically no toxicity but they stimulated the immune system. This was confirmed in the United States where they found that the fruit prevented a breakdown of the immune system during radiation and chemotherapy treatments. Other countries have now taken this up and combine it with other drugs of herbal origin that stimulate the immune system (e.g. *Astralagus*).

**Cherry Laurel** (*Prunus laurocerasus* L.) is the common hedging laurel and although it is not a native it is well established in Britain, having been introduced from Eastern Europe and Asia Minor in 1629. That was part of a fashionable enthusiasm for evergreens, to alleviate the brownness of an English winter. The fashion recurred in the 18th century for creating dark shady glades and walkways, in which to contemplate the Muses. Next, the Victorians included it in their enthusiasm for sombre evergreens and so

Laurel is common nowadays, with some massive specimens and clumps in old gardens, parks, cemeteries and churchyards. It seems to be having a revival, with housing companies planting it for hedging round their closes of new properties. It's a poor choice, despite flourishing in shade. It's a large shrub with large leaves for a large job – no amount of clipping can curtail this to low thin barriers around cramped modern closes. That said, there are now low-growing cultivars on the market but some compensate for a lack of height with an enthusiasm for spreading widely and rapidly, so check for this when buying hedging. The more it has to be cut the more the owners expose themselves to its toxic hydrogen cyanide compounds, by getting the sap on their hands and inhaling the vapours. Hedges should be cut when there is a wind so as to avoid excessive inhalation and if the clippings are burned then the wise work upwind of the bonfire smoke. Gloves should be worn. Laurel foliage is so poisonous that entomologists used to chop up the leaves and put them in their killing jars when preserving caught specimens. More hazards arise when the spikes of strongly scented creamy flowers develop into fruits, changing from green to luscious red and purple and through to black. They look very tempting to children. Birds love them too but quickly evacuate the kernels. Humans should not consume the kernels at all. As for consuming the flesh of the fruit there is debate about its level of toxicity. Certainly the fruit of some trees is far more bitter than on others and the greater the bitterness the greater the risk. There are published recipes for culinary usage but a lot of them are American and it may be that the fruit is less toxic there than here so the wisest action would be to avoid the lot and warn children not to eat them, even if they attract flocks of feeding birds. If children return somewhat excited, with dilated pupils to their eyes, then medical help should be sought, before they develop convulsions or breathing difficulties. The recorded fatalities have been due to respiratory failure. Nevertheless, in the hands of an expert the compounds can be used medicinally to *aid* respiration, as in cases of asthma, coughs and whooping cough. Similarly, controlled amounts can aid the stomach and have been used for dyspepsia, indigestion, nausea and vomiting, while very dilute solutions have been used to bathe infected eyes. It has never been of great medicinal value here because by the time the tree was introduced the British people already had solutions for such problems using native plants. Thus it was not brought into use until 1731, by Madden, in Dublin, following fatalities when it had been used as a substitute for Bitter Almond flavouring. The use of its compound, amygdalin, as such a substitute continued long afterwards. In present times it has been used as an anti-cancer drug although the practice is not recommended currently due to its toxicity.

**Box** (*Buxus Sempervirens* L.) is a native tree but is now extremely local in the wild. In gardens it has been used for hundreds of years, starting probably with the Romans who were using it in their gardens before they even got to Britain. Then there was a lull before its popularity rose again during the 16th and 17th centuries as a low hedging for geometric Renaissance designs. For this they turned to the dwarf edging Box, 'Suffruticosa', which was known to John Gerard in the 16th century but is of unknown date and origin. After that, we started planting Box in 'naturalistic landscapes' to enclose evergreen walks, as per the famous ones on Box Hill, Surrey. Then the Victorians used Box in their enthusiasm for dark brooding evergreens. Thus it can be found commonly in cemeteries and churchyards and occasionally as a small tree in gardens. Recently, it has enjoyed a revival with the fashion for low hedges, clipped shapes and topiary, bringing it once again into common contact with 21st century people. There are 70 species and numerous extra cultivars of Box and these are basically safe in gardens because the little leathery leaves are so unappetising and such a lot would need to be eaten before symptoms of poisoning would show. Even an average sized horse needs to eat nearly a kilogram of clippings before it is in serious trouble. The Victorian enthusiasm for the tree spread beyond gardeners and made this one of the early subjects for pharmacological analysis. By the mid 19th century they had isolated the toxic compound and named it buxine. That analysis has since been refined and produced similar compounds such as parabuxine and parabuxonidine. These belong to a complex group of compounds known as steroidal alkaloids. They will produce stomach pain and vomiting before convulsions and death through respiratory failure, when the foliage is taken as fodder. Nevertheless, we've tried using it in medicines as a laxative and purgative, to reduce fever and to expel intestinal worms but it is not, however, suited to self-medication. It is better to leave it as a decorative evergreen of charm and versatility.

Clipped conifer hedges have traditionally been of **Thuja** of which there are five species in general cultivation and the commonest for hedges is the **Western Red Cedar** (*Thuja plicata*.D..Don), which arrived from Eastern North America in 1853. It's aromatic with essential oils which contain the toxin thujone. These conifers are not much of a hazard in the garden since you would have to eat large amounts before it did you any harm, but don't feed it to the pet rabbit or let livestock browse it. After the mid-20th century came the innovation of informal hedges of attractive flowering and berried shrubs. Some of these came from the Rosaceae family, such as the Rugosa Roses with large blousy, scented blooms, followed by big bright hips full of vitamin C. Leave these on the bushes to feed the winter birds; greenfinches love them. Also in this group is the white-flowering *Pyrancantha*, with yellow-orange and red berry clusters. These have always been considered poisonous but currently it is thought that has been over-emphasised and that it is only mildly toxic. Although it does not pose a major threat it is probably not a good idea to turn the berries into jam!

Let us move on to other trees and shrubs now, from standards in old hedgerows through to shrub borders and feature plantings. Here the choice is vast again, drawn from all round the temperate world, but many of the species have been on offer for a long time and so there is more knowledge of their behaviour in Britain. The families alert us to potential hazards, such as the Leguminoseae with the **Laburnum** and **False Acacia**, and not forgetting the **Wisteria** up the wall. It is the species with berries that are more worrying and quite rightly so. Every autumn the gardening press features a range of colourful berried shrubs to grow for seasonal colour. If children are taught not to eat berries then these won't be a problem. The **Skimmia** (*Skimmia japonica* Thun.) is a smart-growing species with terminal bunches of bright red fruits. Although these are toxic, large amounts need to be eaten before symptoms of poisoning occur and so it is often listed as 'safe'. The toxin, found throughout the plant, is the quinolone alkaloid, skimmianine, which is a muscle poison inducing death through cardiac arrest. Much more dangerous are the smart red berries of the **Daphnes.** The native **Mezereum** (*Daphne mezereum* L.) is the commonest at the garden centres because it produces its starry pink flowers up the bare stems before the leaves appear and therefore has great appeal in the spring when we start thinking about our gardens again. Another scented native Daphne is **Spurge Laurel** (*Daphne laureola* L.) with little bunches of greenish yellow blooms among the evergreen leaves and this too flowers early in the year. It is later, when the berries ripen, that the hazards are most acute, although all parts of the plant are toxic, including the flowers. Having it indoors when in bloom can fill the room with toxic vapours. Simply handling the plant gives some people dermatitis, but often these skin irritations last for only a few minutes. Consumption gives an intense burning pain the mouth which should put off little children. If the berries are swallowed whole, however, poisoning can be much more serious; with fatalities arising from kidney failure. The toxins are a diterpenoid called mezerein and a glycoside called daphnin. There is a long history of using Daphnes in folk medicines and some of these have become official. At present the active compounds are still being investigated as their action seems quite complicated – on the one hand there is work leading to anti-leukaemia treatments while other research has shown that in the presence of certain anti-cancer drugs the Daphne compounds become carcinogenic themselves.

Another tree of the pea family is the **False Acacia** or **Black Locust** (*Robinia psuedoacacia* L.) which is often found in big Victorian gardens and thus occurs where new housing has been infilled, plus the new golden-leaved cultivars have proved popular, both in gardens but also for street planting. All parts of the tree are poisonous but without juicy berries to tempt the unwary instances of human poisoning are rare. Pets like rabbits are at risk if they are exercised in the garden because the tree sends up suckers from its roots, often many metres from the trunk, and these can get nibbled. Where these suckers can arise beyond the boundary into a pasture, or along a hedgerow, they are a major hazard to livestock. Horses are said to be affected ten times more severely than cattle; poultry are affected also. The rich scent of the trusses of white blooms attracts bees and there is debate over the toxicity of the honey. Some reports say it is contaminated with the toxins while some apiarists say it is one of the best of honeys. Fortunately British bees usually forage a wide variety of plants over a considerable area and so honey produced commercially is thoroughly mixed, thereby diluting any toxicity.

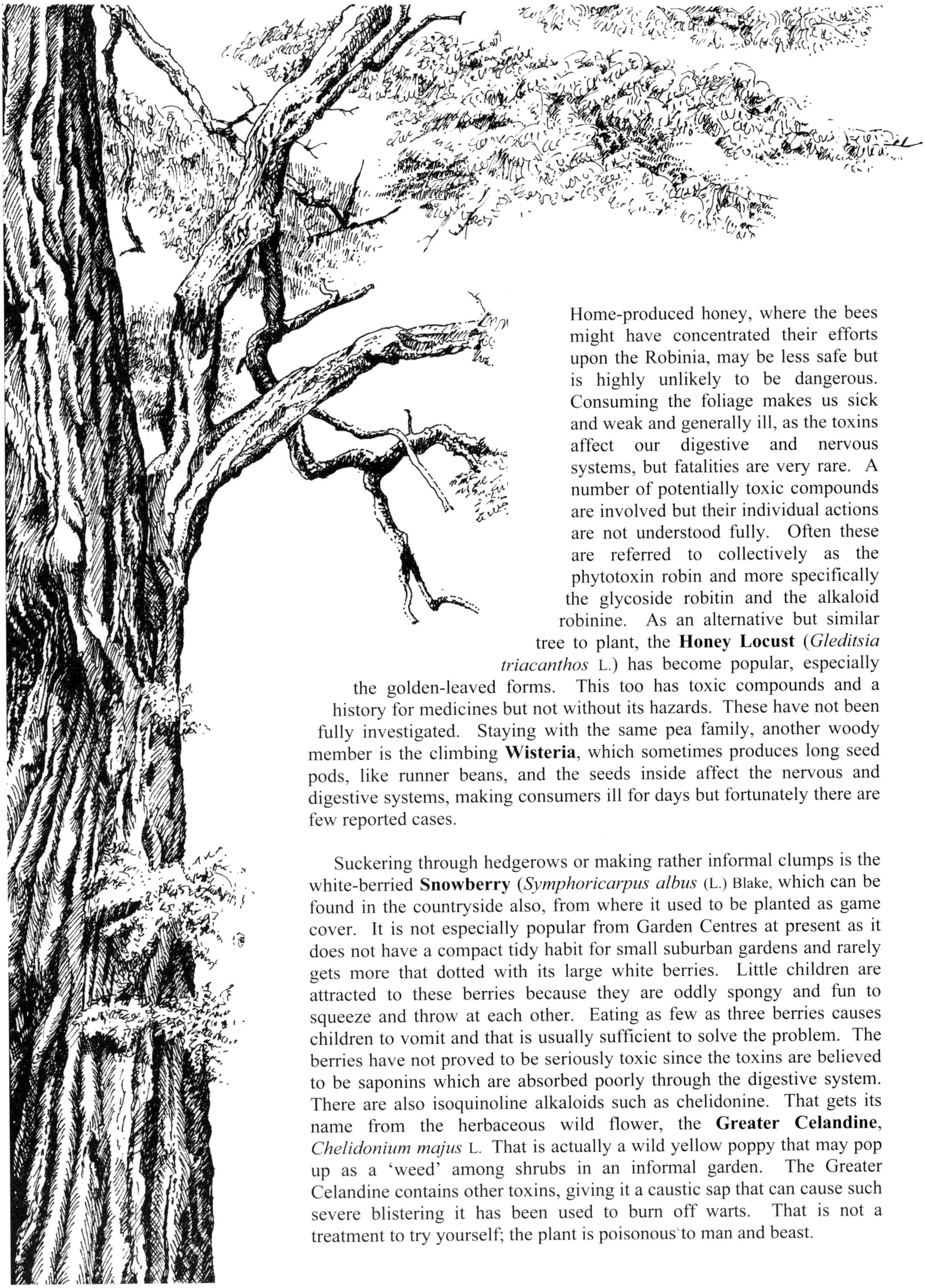

Home-produced honey, where the bees might have concentrated their efforts upon the Robinia, may be less safe but is highly unlikely to be dangerous. Consuming the foliage makes us sick and weak and generally ill, as the toxins affect our digestive and nervous systems, but fatalities are very rare. A number of potentially toxic compounds are involved but their individual actions are not understood fully. Often these are referred to collectively as the phytotoxin robin and more specifically the glycoside robitin and the alkaloid robinine. As an alternative but similar tree to plant, the **Honey Locust** (*Gleditsia triacanthos* L.) has become popular, especially the golden-leaved forms. This too has toxic compounds and a history for medicines but not without its hazards. These have not been fully investigated. Staying with the same pea family, another woody member is the climbing **Wisteria**, which sometimes produces long seed pods, like runner beans, and the seeds inside affect the nervous and digestive systems, making consumers ill for days but fortunately there are few reported cases.

Suckering through hedgerows or making rather informal clumps is the white-berried **Snowberry** (*Symphoricarpus albus* (L.) Blake, which can be found in the countryside also, from where it used to be planted as game cover. It is not especially popular from Garden Centres at present as it does not have a compact tidy habit for small suburban gardens and rarely gets more that dotted with its large white berries. Little children are attracted to these berries because they are oddly spongy and fun to squeeze and throw at each other. Eating as few as three berries causes children to vomit and that is usually sufficient to solve the problem. The berries have not proved to be seriously toxic since the toxins are believed to be saponins which are absorbed poorly through the digestive system. There are also isoquinoline alkaloids such as chelidonine. That gets its name from the herbaceous wild flower, the **Greater Celandine**, *Chelidonium majus* L. That is actually a wild yellow poppy that may pop up as a 'weed' among shrubs in an informal garden. The Greater Celandine contains other toxins, giving it a caustic sap that can cause such severe blistering it has been used to burn off warts. That is not a treatment to try yourself; the plant is poisonous to man and beast.

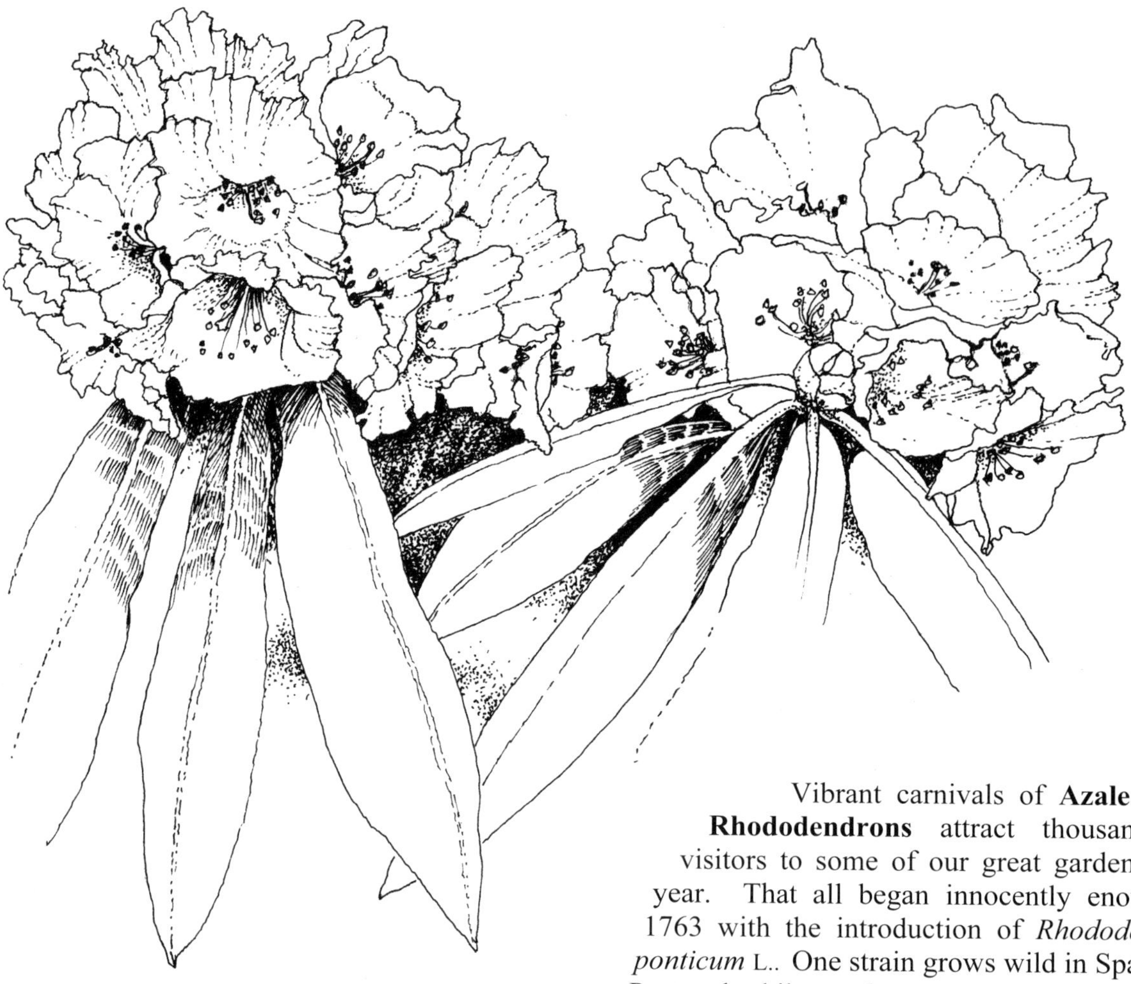

Vibrant carnivals of **Azaleas** and **Rhododendrons** attract thousands of visitors to some of our great gardens each year. That all began innocently enough in 1763 with the introduction of *Rhododendron ponticum* L.. One strain grows wild in Spain and Portugal while another grows at the eastern end of the Mediterranean, as at Pontus in Turkey (hence the name ponticum). It soon found the British Isles to its liking and became a prime plant in so many of our great country estates. Then it began to show its true character – spreading vigorously by seed and suppressing all competitors without compassion, by casting deep shade throughout the year and by releasing poisons into the soil. Very few plants will grow among established Rhododendrons. Soon great swathes of them were sweeping through woodlands and by the second half of the 20th century it was realised, rather late, that they were in fact destroying our natural woodlands by preventing natural regeneration. Getting rid of them was more easily said than done. They have proved to be veritably indestructible and the name *Rhododenron ponticum* became satanic. In truth this species is a great rarity in Britain. The menace on the rampage is a collection of hybrids, giving rise to great variation in colour and flowering time. These arose initially from cross-breeding with other introductions, such as *Rhododendron catawbiense,* which had been introduced from the Appalachians in 1809, and gave rise to fertile hybrids. Indeed this was a species much used by nurserymen to increase the range of garden hybrids, of which the most famous and widely planted were those of the Waterer family at their Woking nursery in Surrey. However, this species should not be given all the 'blame' since plant collectors were introducing dozens of species from North America and the Far East to satisfy the fashion for these shrubs in the 19th century. Consequently, there is a great diversity of genetic material in the 'wild' stock of Britain. The whole plant is toxic – it even kills earthworms that venture too close – but there is natural variation between the world's species and thus in the hybrids running amok in Britain. The aerial parts contain toxic resins which are known collectively as andromedotoxins, or more commonly now, as grayanotoxin. Humans are rarely tempted to eat it but these compounds can contaminate honey and then they cause a reaction known as grayanotoxin poisoning, honey intoxication, mad honey intoxication or simply Rhododendron poisoning. Symptoms are stomach upsets and vomiting which is usually warning enough and the patient usually recovers within 24 hours without medical aid. Particularly high intakes do lead to further bodily disturbances but occurrences are very rare. Poisoning from commercial British honey is most unlikely to arise but cases do occur from foreign honey, from countries like Turkey where the problem was first described way back in 401 BCE.

Rhododendrons are hazardous because they have escaped into the wild and therefore are not under such close supervision as in our gardens where their toxic leaves are far less likely to be eaten by browsing animals. In our gardens we have other ericaceous plants from around the world plus other shrubs that associate well with them, like the Magnolias. By late Victorian times they were very much the vogue for gardens on sandy acid soils and so, by now, surviving plantings have matured and their flamboyance when in bloom attracts thousands of visitors. Among the other shrubs associating with them are some that are notoriously toxic in their homelands but do not cause problems in our gardens. One example is the **Calico Bush** (*Kalmia*) of which there are seven species in the genus. The commonest in gardens is *Kalmia latifolia* L. which was an early introduction in this category, in 1734, and a good choice for the garden since it is less demanding of moisture than some of the other species, which grow in peat bogs. *Kalmia angustifolia* L. (introduced 1736) is one and has naturalised into British peat bogs, both in North West and South East England. Another is *Kalmia polifolia* Wangenh., (introduced 1767) which is more likely to be found in the bogs of South East England but both these species may be encountered in gardens. In this group of plants look out also for the **Lily of the Valley Tree** from the genus *Pieris* of which three species are popular: *P. floribunda, japonica* and *formosa.* Again they have histories of toxicity when grazed as wild shrubs in the wild. In our gardens they should be safe from browsers and our cats and dogs are no more likely to eat them than we are. Finally, we can overlook the **Pernettyas** which were in the genus *Pernettya* but which are now classified as *Gaultheria.* Their flowers are inconspicuous but once fertilised develop into beautiful little berries that can range from white through pinks and lilac to crimson and purple. Birds don't like them so they stay on the low shrubs all winter. Children do like them though. They are spongy but tough so they are fun to squeeze and throw at each other – much more fun than eating them. The juice on their hands is not a major hazard as the berries are only very mildly poisonous and a lot would have to be eaten before suffering stomach upsets.

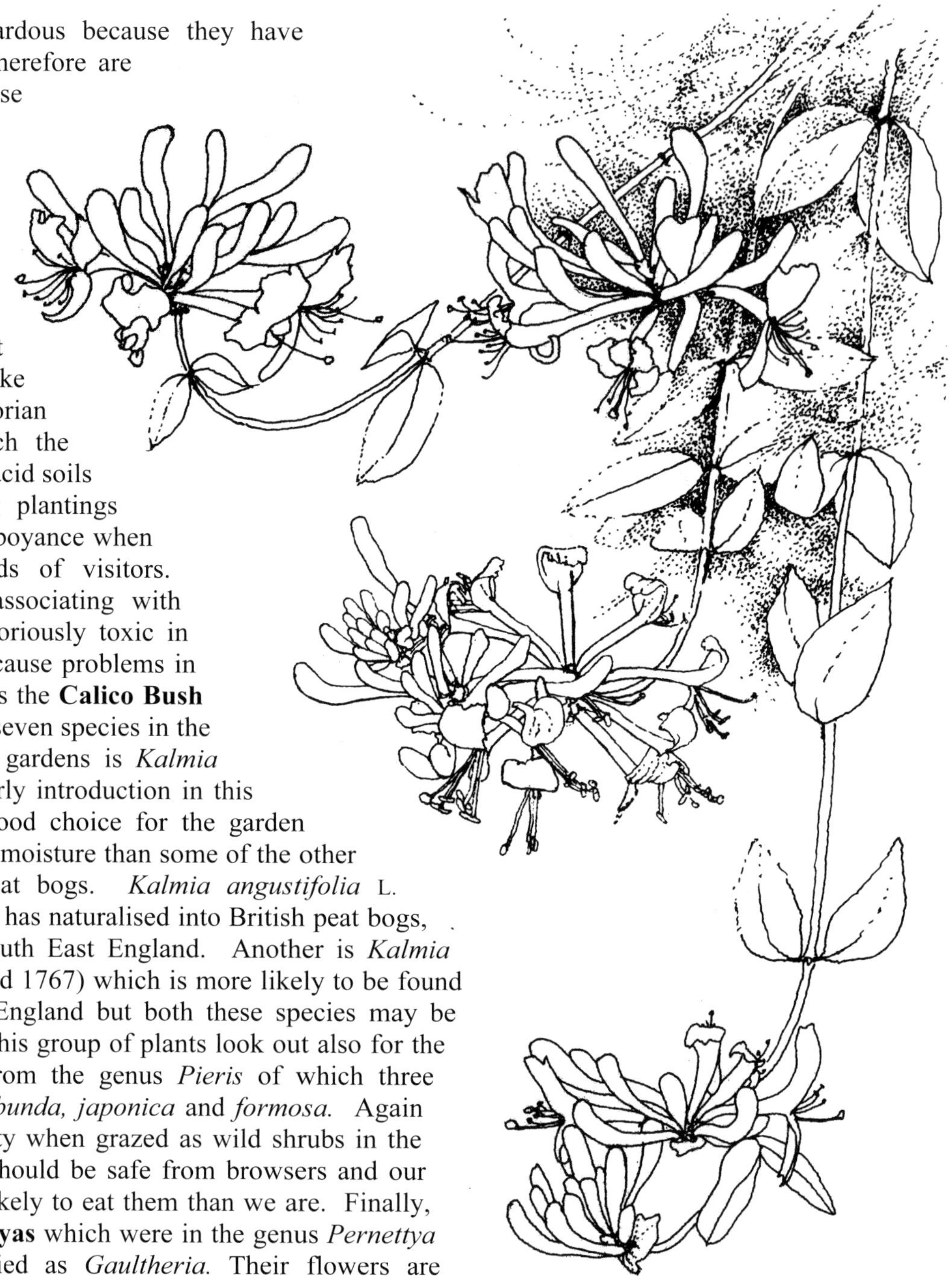

Far more commonly grown are the **Honeysuckles**, of which there are about 180 in the genus *Lonicera.* One species is native to Britain but many of the others are grown here in gardens. Of these, at least fourteen have been recorded as naturalised into the wild as 'garden escapes' and some have become well established for decades. We tend to think of these as climbing shrubs, due to the popularity of the native Wild Honeysuckle or **Woodbine** (*Lonicera periclymenum* L.) but some of the genus are shrubby and *Lonicera nitida* Wils. is often used for hedging; its golden-leaved cultivar has become fashionable as a foliage plant. To confuse matters further, some of the climbing species have been developed into garden cultivars that are mound forming. Thus Honeysuckles do not always look like the British Wild Honeysuckle illustrated here and some of the introduced species may be encountered in the wild. Some have red berries while others have purplish or black. Buying one at

the garden centre can be confusing too if the label only gives the cultivar name and not the species from which it was developed. The very popular 'Graham Thomas' was selected from the native species by the horticulturalist of that name, who spotted a particularly fine strain growing in a hedgerow and took cuttings. This species has always been considered poisonous, especially the shiny bright red berries, which do look very tempting, but recent evaluations have decreed that the plant is only mildly toxic and even if children eat a few of the berries it is not crisis time. They are likely to cause vomiting and diarrhoea but in general little work has been done on the toxicity of Honeysuckles. It is thought that the symptoms of poisoning are caused by saponins.

In the same family as the Honeysuckles, Caprifoliaceae, are the Viburnums of which the two British species, The Wayfaring Tree and the Guelder Rose, often raise questions about possible toxicity. They contain viburnine but again are considered safe as levels are so low. The **Guelder Rose** (*Viburnum opulus* L.), of which there are garden cultivars, has beautiful clusters of shiny red berries which droop in an attractive way and hint at lusciousness. Squeeze one and you will be disappointed. It will be hard since the skin covers the seed with no flesh to eat. Nevertheless they have been used as food in the past, in jellies and preserves etc. but would have provided little more than only flavouring. Even so, in North America where it grows also, it was used regularly by the Iroquois, Shuswap and Ojibwa nations. The berries do contain active ingredients which leaves a large question mark over possible toxicity, although this does not seem to be proven and no case studies could be traced. The traditional wisdom is that eating them raw makes you feel unwell but cooking them renders them safe; best left to please the eye rather than the stomach. The same can be said for that other Viburnum, the **Wayfaring Tree** (*Viburnum lantana* L.) but the little hard berries are far less tempting. Decidedly unappetising are the fruits of the **Strawberry Tree** (*Arbutus unedo* L.), named after the appearance of the fruits, not the flavour. They worry people over possible toxicity but fear not; only the fruits are likely to be eaten and these are deemed to be so mildly toxic as to be 'safe.' Although its name, *unedo*, means we only eat one, that refers to it being so unappetising rather than drop-dead dangerous.

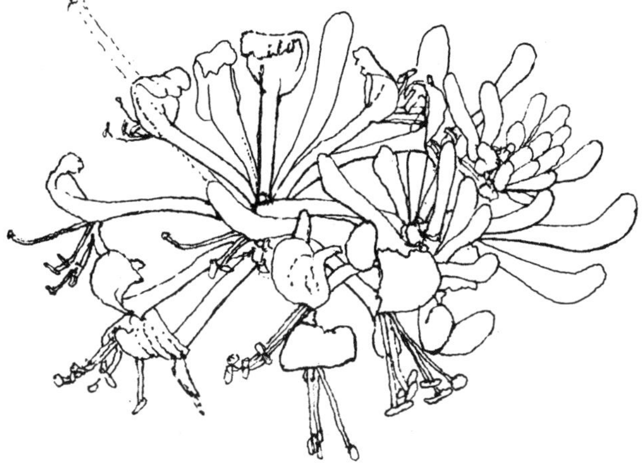

The **Laburnum** (*Laburnum anagyroides* Medikus) is so beautiful when in flower and was introduced for this reason, from Central and Southern Europe in 1560. Then in 1596 arrived a second species, the **Scotch Laburnum** (*Laburnum alpinum* Bercht. and Presl.), also from Southern Europe. In both cases all parts of the tree are poisonous, with the seeds being responsible for the vast majority of cases of poisoning in humans. Fortunately it is now one of the better known of our poisonous plants, following media publicity in the 20th century - in 1979 some 3,000 children were admitted to hospital with Laburnum poisoning. That does not mean they all *needed* hospital treatment. There is still debate as to just out susceptible are children to the toxins in Laburnum. On the one hand we can read that it takes only two seeds to kill a child and on the other hand we can read that the danger has been exaggerated grossly. Although the seeds taste nasty, they are small and easily swallowed. They act first as an irritant, causing vomiting, leading on to in-coordination, drowsiness, convulsions, coma and death due to respiratory failure. The toxins are quinolizidine alkaloids, such as cytosine – lethal, but useful. Researchers have explored its analgesic qualities and the effects on the brain (it acts like nicotine and has been investigated for usefulness in treating addictions, such as to nicotine). Considerable variation between trees has been reported and also that each can vary seasonally. As the seeds mature so their toxicity increases while at this time the toxicity in the rest of tree decreases. Variation will arise also from hybridisation and this does occur in Britain between the two species. The hybrid was brought to attention in 1864, in a Surrey garden, and developed for commerce by Waterers Nursery at Woking. Thus it was sold as *Laburnum x watereri* but is now known as *L. vossii*. It is often said to be safer but that lies in the fewer number of pods it produces - the seeds inside are just as dangerous.

**Underplanting and Border Plants**

Let us move on from the trees and shrubs to the underplanting, which again involves many plants from the woodlands and sunny glades, including a number of native species. These have become scarce in the wild and are far more likely to be encountered at the Garden Centres. None has been more important than the **Lily of the Valley** (*Convallaria majalis* L.) not only as a garden desirable but as a crop for supplying the French perfume industry. In the spring is sends up massed juicy bright green spears that must be very tempting to any deer or woodland forager so it is no surprise that these are laced with active compounds. They affect the heart. This we have learnt to exploit to our advantage. The chief compounds of interest are glycosides such as convallarin and convallamarin but you will find a whole host of related compounds listed, totalling about forty. This simple elegant plant is very complicated. The compounds slow down the heart beat and make it more regular, while at the same time act as a diuretic to stimulate the removal of surplus fluid from the blood, to increase the efficiency of the heart. They are therefore valuable when the patient has high blood pressure. The body does this without demanding extra supplies of oxygen so the systems are not put under strain. Thus the drug acts like digitalin from Foxgloves but it is much safer, especially for ageing patients because the compounds are far less cumulative; being more readily excreted through the kidneys. Their absorption rate is low which gives the kidneys more time to deal with them, especially as the compounds are released into the blood in sequence rather than in a rush. Lily of the Valley can be used in conjunction with compounds derived from Hawthorn fruits, to good effect. Get it wrong and Lily of the Valley causes nausea and vomiting and slowing of the heart to a dangerous level; fatalities are reported. The treatment to counteract those symptoms can be atropine from Deadly Nightshade, which has the reverse effects. Lily of

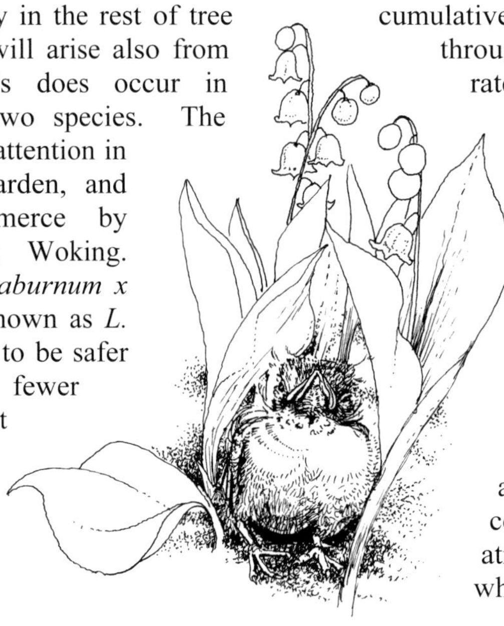

the Valley affects the central nervous system too and can be sedative and anti-convulsant, useful in the treatment of epilepsy and palsy. Wonderful as it is, this plant is dangerous. Indeed it contains some of the most lethal heart toxins to be found in plants and should not be used for home-made treatments. Its use is restricted by law, under the Medicines Act (1968), to professionals who are qualified appropriately to administer such drugs. The whole plant is toxic, including the red berries, but especially the flowers. Accidental cases of human poisoning are very rare. If used as a cut flower it is probably wise to dispose of the vase water with care since there is a tradition that the toxins leach into it but some modern tests have failed to prove this.

For attractive evergreen plantings the Hellebores are excellent, especially the two native species, the **Green Hellebore** (*Helleborus viridis* L.) and the **Stinking Hellebore** (*Helleborus foetidus* L.). To these we have added the ever popular **Christmas Rose** (*Helleborus niger* L.) which came from Central and Southern Europe and Western Asia and was introduced in the 16th century. Then in 1839 was introduced the **Lenten Rose** (*Helleborus orientalis* L.) from Greece and this is the one plant breeders have worked so hard upon to give a massive range of colour variations today. All are toxic and that involves the whole plant, including the flowers which can lead to contamination of honey. There are variations between the species but basically they contain glycosides that affect the heart, such as hellebrigenin and hellebrin. There are also saponosides such as helleborine and helleborem. Then for good measure there is the lactone heteroside, protoanemonine, because the Hellebores belong to the Rannunculaceae. The cardinolide compounds accelerate the heart and have been used as heart stimulants for the elderly but that has now been superseded by safer drugs. Treatment for poisoning requires the heart to be slowed down again and so can include atropine from the Deadly Nightshade. Poisoning in humans is rare due to the burning taste of the protoanemonine but consumption leads to digestive upset and vomiting. Then the various compounds affect the nervous system, acting not only upon the heart but respiration, so that in severe cases there can be delirium and convulsions before death from heart and respiratory failure. Be careful handling these plants since the toxins can be absorbed through the skin. In particular rolling the seeds out of the pods by hand pushes the compounds into the skin. Although the Hellebores have a long history in medicine for a wide range of problems they are nevertheless dangerous and should be used only by qualified practitioners. (Both illus. *H. niger*)

A producer of red berries is that botanical curiosity, the **Butcher's Broom** (*Ruscus aculeatus* L.), a low evergreen woodland shrub that shows up well in the winter. In early autumn it ripens bright scarlet berries, the size of a small cherry, which are borne singly in the centre of what look like sharply-pointed leaves but which are really rigid flattened shoots (cladodes). The young shoots have been eaten as a substitute for Asparagus, to which it is related, but which inspired Hulme's observation that it looks "about as tempting a delicacy as scrap-iron." Do not harvest the shoots as this is not a very common plant and in any case they are not a worthy substitute for Asparagus and they do contain active ingredients. These are still exploited in herbal medicines; added, for example, to some Horse Chestnut Extract products for the treatment of varicose veins to increase the elasticity of the veins and thereby the function of their valves. It is used in other treatments too but should be taken only under qualified medical supervision due to its toxic action. Children could be tempted to pick and eat the berries, especially as they taste sweet, at first, then turn bitter. Consumption causes vomiting, so the toxins are soon voided, and diarrhoea will follow but large consumptions lead to convulsions.

For underplanting in moist shade, again on alkaline soils, our native **Herb Paris** (*Paris quadifolia* L.) is planted sometimes, for its distinctive foliage and green flowers. The fruits are black berries. Children might eat them but the toxins are saponins (paristyphnine and paridine), so they are absorbed poorly into the system and although the child will be unwell it is unlikely to be able to find enough berries in a garden, or even in the wild, to develop severe symptoms. The saponins are not lethal.

The **Roast Beef Plant** (*Iris foetidissima L.*) is one of our two native Irises and has become popular for its autumn colour: the three-part seed pods split open to reveal double rows of brilliant orange berries. If consumed, these will cause stomach irritation and even bleeding but patients recover in a few days. The main toxic area is the rhizome. The plant is so named for the smell of its juice. This is not a modern day roast beef smell but from former times when beef could be putrefying, hence it's other name of **Stinking Iris**. That name has been dropped in Garden Centres as it lacks commercial appeal. It grows well in shade, and dry shade at that, with the additional advantage of liking alkaline soils. It does not stink noticeably when growing in the shade but the sun catches one of mine at flowering time, resulting in a smell of carrion, presumably to attract flies for pollination. Getting the sap of this and the **Flag Irises** of the borders onto skin can make it sensitive to light, producing nasty wounds, so wear gloves when dividing Irises.

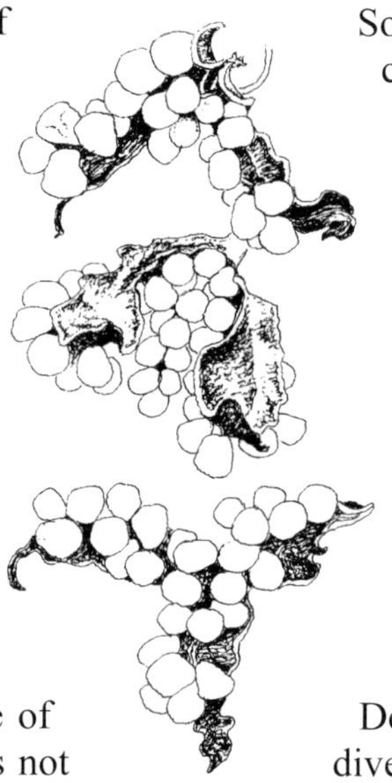

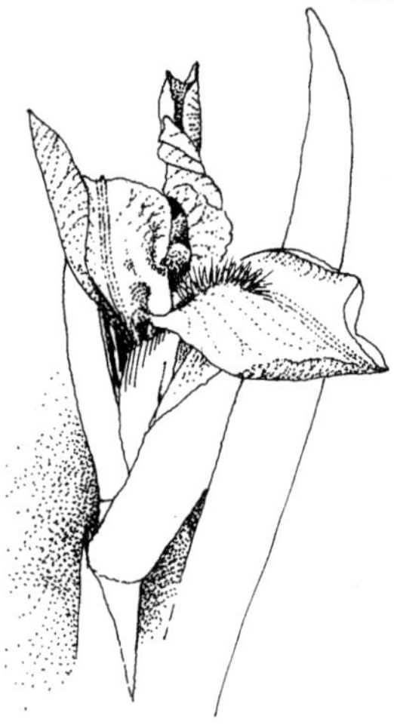

By the time the Irises are going over the **Delphiniums** are raising their flower spikes with an air of expectation of their stately spires. There are over 250 species in the genus, spread right round the North Temperate zone, with outliers isolated in African mountains. Where they grow wild they cause severe economic losses by killing livestock that graze them but Britain has no native species to worry stock-holders. A few species have escaped from gardens into the wild but do not occur so profusely as to be a hazard – a lethal dose for a cow would be about 3kg. Cattle are the most susceptible, with sheep the least. Loss of cattle is so serious in countries like the United States that vets have developed an aversion therapy to train the cattle not to eat these plants. Apparently this works perfectly until untrained cattle are introduced to the herd and then the trained ones abandon their education and go back to eating Delphiniums.

Some Delphiniums are annual, like that old cottage garden favourite, the **Larkspur**, while others are biennial but it's the perennial species that come to mind with the name Delphinium. Traditionally they have been in a wide range of blues, violets, white and pink. The genus is unusual for having all three primary colours among its species. Plant breeders in recent years have turned to the red species to try and breed the genes into the familiar garden hybrids in order to extend the colour range of the tall garden hybrids. Consequently the Delphiniums in our gardens today can be diverse and have a wide genetic make-up, rather than just the long established hybrids for which the chief parent was *Delphinium elatum* L. It is important to remember this diversity so as not to overlook potential hazards. The genus belongs to the Buttercup family, the Ranunculaceae, which has been encountered several times in this book, for harbouring caustic toxins of the proto-anemonine group, but the Delphiniums are far more heavily defended. From the nine species most often responsible for livestock fatalities over forty toxins have been identified. The virulent alkaloids kill people too. Fortunately much of the danger is concentrated in the little dry blackish brown seeds that do not look appetising to humans. The foliage is far less toxic and this decreases as the plant ages – by the time the seeds are maturing the toxic levels in the rest of the plant have dropped to just one sixteenth of what they were when the shoots first rose in the spring. Gardeners who try to grow Delphiniums will rue the fact these toxins do not deter slugs and snails. Beware of excessive handing of the shoots in the spring, if dividing up mature crowns or taking a lot of cuttings, since the toxins can be absorbed through the skin. Symptoms of poisoning start with stomach upsets and then with a mood change as the toxins affect the brain, producing a sense of nervous unease and depression, followed by tiredness and muscle spasms until ultimately death can result from respiratory failure. The toxins are diterpenoid alkaloids, which act as neuromuscular blocking agents and include delphinine, delphineidine and ajacine. The seeds contain calcatripine, which has been used as a vermifuge to kill head lice etc. In general the Delphiniums are too toxic to have a long history of medical use, and there are usually safer alternative treatments today.

The Delphiniums are far more virulent than the other members of the Ranunculaceae profiled so far, but another genus in the family far excels even Delphiniums. This is the genus *Aconitum* for the **Monkshoods**. There are about a hundred species of which one is considered native to Britain: *Aconitum napellus* L., which is still referred to regularly as *A. anglicum.* It is rare in the wild although garden escapes crop up widely, in moist shady places. So do specimens that are hybrids between the other species grown in gardens. Whereas the Delphiniums have the distinctive spur projecting behind the flower (see topmost flower buds in the illus.) the Monkshoods have a hood petal that comes forwards over the bloom – very tightly in the British species (as per the illus. overleaf) but less close-fitting and often distinctly beautiful in foreign species. Whether growing wild or in gardens, the Monkshoods are among our few drop-dead-dangerous plants and are a major hazard currently, due to sustained promotion by the horticulture industry over the last few years. The range is even greater because the plant breeders have been busy developing new garden cultivars. Indeed these perennials are very beautiful with their tall straight stems, cut or lobed leaves and large intense purple-blue flowers. There are also white and blue-and-white versions, plus variation in the shape of the flowers but they all have the distinctive hooded petal over the top. Some bloom in early summer while others wait until late summer/early autumn. The most virulent are the Japanese species and probably the hybrids containing their genes. Although they have the same toxins as the European they are more potent. Treat them all with the greatest care.

It is quite astonishing how the horticulture industry avoids all mention of the toxicity. This spring nine different suppliers sent me catalogues that made a feature of these plants and they all ignored the issue. Even worse, five of them promoted Monkshood as good cut-flowers. Beware, they can fill the room with noxious fumes. Some readers may remember a News bulletin, some years ago, announcing that a florist and her staff had been rushed to Intensive Care after being overcome by the scent of flowers in their shop. The problem was traced to a consignment of cut-flowers received from Holland that included Monkshood. These florists needed Intensive Care for several days but modern science did save them. The next night there was a further News bulletin, saying another florist, who on hearing the previous, had realised she too had Monkshood among her cut-flowers and had rushed down to the shop to banish them to the back room until they could be dealt with the next morning. However, when she entered that back room the next day, she too was overcome. Some species of *Aconitum* are more toxic than others and again the level is variable, but obviously this is not a plant with which to take chances. Having related these stories when tutoring a course on poisonous plants I was utterly amazed the next week when a student entered bearing beautiful blue flowers, saying, "This is Monkshood isn't it?" Do take notice of the above; there must be better ways to get featured on the News.

The genus *Aconitum* belongs to the family Ranunculaceae which has been featured several times in this book already, in terms of them containing caustic compounds of the protoanemonine group. The genus *Aconitum,* however, goes further in its chemical armoury. Members contain two groups of alkaloids: the aconitine group which includes aconitine itself and neopelline, and the pseudoaconitine group which includes pseudoaconintine and bikaconitine. The roots, which can have tubers, are the most heavily defended. These have catecholamine alkaloids, quaternary ammonium compounds, isoquinolines, and more. Obviously this lot has diverse actions in our bodies but basically they attack the heart and nervous system, dramatically. In herbal medicines the Monkshoods have a history going back over two thousand years and it has not ended yet. In many cases though, the treatments now rely upon safer substitutes, since it is so difficult to determine a stimulating dose of aconitine from a lethal one. Fortunately, if a casualty can be kept alive for 24 hours the outlook is encouraging because the digestive system will by then have metabolised the alkaloids into safer compounds and these are eliminated rapidly. Even so, it takes days and days to recover and specialised treatment. If Monkshood poisoning is suspected then medical help should be sought immediately. Eating the little tubers has caused fatalities in the past but today the main options for exposure are likely to arise from using them as a cut-flower and from absorbing the juice through the hands when gardening.

Let's stay with the Ranunculaceae and turn to those magnificent 'buttercups', the **Peonies.** These have long been thought of as highly toxic but this is not really the case. Certainly they do contain active compounds which have been used in medicines for over two thousand years but in terms of safe gardening and cut-flowers they do not pose a significant hazard. They are not for eating though. That might sound frivolous but in their history, species like *Paeonia officinalis* L. (illus. above) have been used as flavouring. The beautiful big glossy black seeds were ground up as a spice, especially when imported spices were taxed. The seeds were used whole for decorating milk puddings too. The plant's name '*officinalis* tells us it was an official medicine too. The first medicinal *Paeonia* to be introduced was probably the single *P. mascula,* (illus. left) which is now one of our rarest wild flowers. As its name suggests, it was brought in to solve men's problems. That upset the ladies who went and brought back one of their own which they said was for women's problems and named it *P. femina.* Theirs worked better than the men's and so that became the official medicine and its names was changed to *P. officinalis*. It always had a high reputation for promoting menstruation and this should be remembered today if it is included in a herbal treatment so that the medicine is not taken by anyone pregnant. Its use has declined since the 16th century but it might crop up in a herbal remedy, perhaps as an antispasmodic for the intestines. For hundreds of years its sedative action was used against epilepsy but that too has now been superseded. Despite this long history and varied applications, ranging from whooping cough to haemorrhoids, the plant has been little studied by modern pharmacology. Quite large amounts need to be consumed before symptoms of poisoning start – the usual stomach upsets lead to vomiting etc. and cases are rare. Children have been known to eat the fallen petals and it only takes a few of these to cause poisoning. The modern border Peonies are derived on the whole from *P. lactiflora Pall.* and that is so mild it is not worth worrying about. Just enjoy the blooms for their all too fleeting season.

Keeping the Peonies company at flowering time are the ever-popular **Columbines** (*Aquilegia*) but they attract attention much earlier in the year when they are among the first herbaceous plant to send up their leaves after Christmas. How attractive are those lobed leaves and unusual among spring greens for being glaucous and tinged with pinky-purple. Our ancestors pounced on those as vegetables for the cooking pot and indeed they are rich in vitamin C – just what was needed when so many people used to suffer from scurvy by the end of the winter. Thus the Columbine became an official source of the vitamin. Then in the 18th century doubt was cast on its safety. Regardless of that, we carried on using it for another hundred years before agreeing, reluctantly, that it was toxic and relegated it to an ingredient for rat bait. That said, it may not have been effective since there are no records of fatalities among mammals and that includes humans. The toxins are destroyed by heat and so adding it to the cooking pot was not a hazard if the meal was heated through properly. However, it was also added to fresh salads and that was not such a good idea. Treat all this with caution though because the pharmacology of this genus is being looked at afresh and increasing the list of compounds therein. It is far more complex than the protoanemonine found in so many other members of the Ranunculaceae. This one contains cyanogenic glycosides, about which little is known, not even whether they are carcinogenic, so do not consume. When they are so beautiful in the garden who wants to eat them anyway?

Leaving this family aside let's move along the herbaceous border, to the pea family again and start worrying about **Lupins** (*Lupinus*). Garden versions have always been considered poisonous and it is best to keep thinking that way. However, not *all* the Lupins are poisonous. Some have been grown for food for several thousand years while others are only just beginning their careers as commercial crops. Some are grown as field crops for animal fodder and some for the oil in their seeds but even these exploitations have proven fatal. It seems as though you really have to know what you are growing and how to treat them when it comes to Lupins. They can also be seen growing *en masse* for reclaiming soil fertility where, for example, pits have been filled and capped with subsoil. So with some 200 members in the genus *Lupinus,* plus the results of hybridization, the situation is quite complex. The horticulture industry is promoting new material, such as Annual Lupins, but the seed packet may not state which species are involved so checking safety is a problem. The range of alkaloids and other toxins through this genus is extensive so wisest counsel is to treat them all as poisonous.

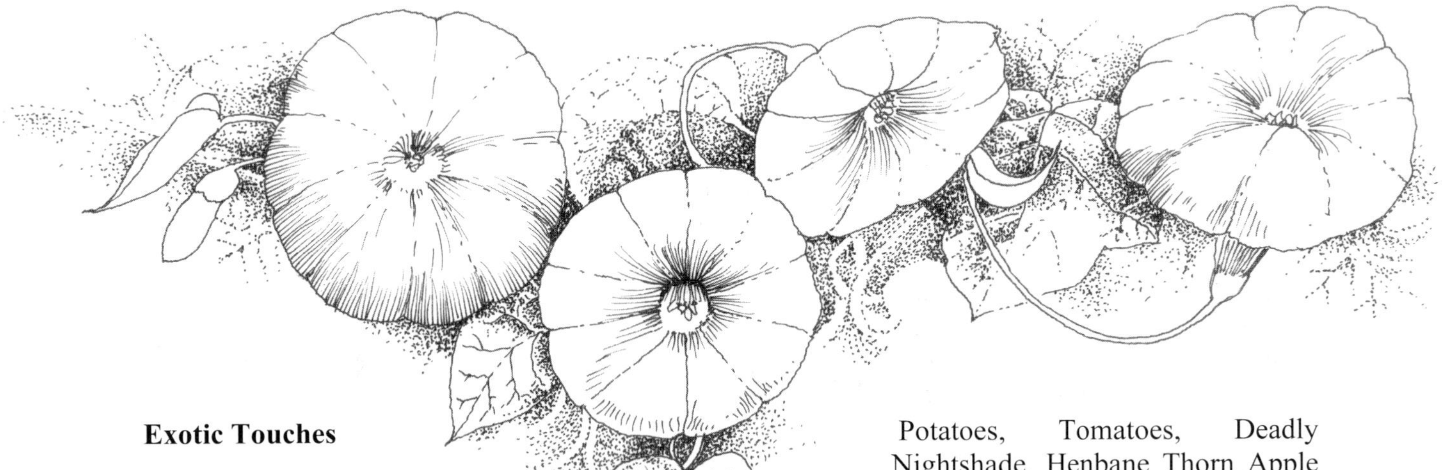

**Exotic Touches**

The horticulture industry has been busy popularising the tropical touch, encouraged by climate change, the fashion for conservatories, and the quest for something new. Nobody thought of growing Bananas when I was a child; the Castor Oil Plant was a novelty and Morning Glory was more or less restricted to people with a heated greenhouse in which to get them started as they were not then a Garden Centre commonplace. In fact there were no Garden Centres as we understand them now. Plants were bought from nurseries. The idea of containerised plants was introduced from the United States in 1958.

**Morning Glory**, is derived from *Ipomoea tricolor* Cav.. This tender annual looks just like the dreaded Greater Bindweed, except that its trumpets are a brilliant sky-blue (although now with colour variations). Both the Bindweed and the Morning Glory belong to the convolvulus family and this is one of only three families of plants in the world that contain virulent poisons called tropanes. The Bindweed is safe but the Morning Glory is not. It's the seeds that are particularly dangerous, so if you open the packet in the kitchen be mighty careful not to spill them. Once again these tropanes can be exploited in many beneficial ways, such as those from *Ipomoea pes-capru* being used to neutralise the venoms of certain jellyfish.

The second family with tropanes is the Erythroxylaceae of the tropics, and so not of direct concern here, although it contains the two trees that yield cocaine and thus it does make an impact upon British society. The third family is big, with over 2,600 members and that is the Solanaceae, met already with Potatoes, Tomatoes, Deadly Nightshade, Henbane Thorn Apple and now the **Angels' Trumpets** (*Brugmansia*) which used to be sold as *Datura.* There are five species and the one commonly grown is *Brugmansia arborea* (L.) Lagerh., introduced from Peru/Chile in 1813. They feature regularly in the mail order catalogues as big exotic pot plants for patio and conservatory where they are strongly scented in the evening. All parts of the plant are toxic if ingested, and that includes smoking the dried leaves to get hallucinatory effects. Apparently there is no pleasure in this and young Americans who try it once, never try it again and warn their friends off. The prime tropanes are atropine, scopolamine, and hyoscyamine, which as usual close down the bodily systems until death results from heart/lung failure.

The fashion for the tropical look has encouraged the growing of the **Castor Oil Plant** (*Ricinus communis* L.) as a feature plant in summer bedding. It also pops up each year in odd places as a seasonal casual. This is the plant that is of economic importance for yielding castor oil and suddenly became famous for yielding the deadly poison, ricin, which hit the News when details were found in a terrorist's notebook. There have also been reports that quantities were actually found in Al Qaeda caves in Afghanistan. Previously there had been reported suspicions that it had been used in the 1980s Iran/Iraq war and back in 1978 this was the poison used in London to kill the Bulgarian writer Georgi Markov by injecting the poison into him 'accidentally' with an adapted umbrella. The plant belongs to the Euphorbia family, along with Spurges and Poinsettias, which have caustic sap, but the Castor Oil Plant goes far beyond causticity and consumption and inhalation must be avoided at all costs. Only a tiny amount can be lethal. Ricin is one of

those compounds that affect our very cells. It gets inside them and stops them making proteins, without which they cannot perpetuate themselves and so the whole body system goes into decline. Without urgent medical help this can be fatal. Obviously there is a delay before the poisoning becomes apparent and so this suits terrorists very nicely and with that in mind no further details are going to be given here, save to say that the cellular action has been explored as a possible way of killing cancer cells and it has also been used in bone marrow transplants.

**Oleanders** have become very popular but the name is applied to two species from different genera. The Common or Pink Oleander is *Nerium oleander* L. while the Yellow Oleander is *Thevetia peruviana* (Pers.) Schum. for which there is also a white-flowered form. Although they belong to different genera they belong to the same family and can be treated as one in terms of toxicity. They are lethal. The toxins are powerful glycosides, such as oleandrin and nerioside, that are carried in the sap and therefore the whole plant poses a hazard. The poisons affect the heart, in much the same way as the toxins found in Foxgloves, but are far more virulent and have some distinct differences. The degree to which a casualty is affected varies also. Do not consume any. Apparently the taste is foul and extremely bitter ('much like a rotten lemon' says one source but how many of us have experience of rotten lemons?) and it causes nausea and vomiting. Heat and fire release the toxins so do not inhale the smoke from burning clippings on a bonfire, nor use it as fuel if cooking out of doors nor use the twigs as meat skewers. There is even a suggestion that it will poison a compost heap if clippings are added and that it poisons the soil in which it is growing. Dead leaves and wilted clippings are just as dangerous since the toxins do not degrade through drying. Take care when tending these beauties not to bruise the tissue so that sap is released and should this happen then wash hands and arms very thoroughly. On the more cheerful side, Oleanders have been explored for medicines and there are many different claims for the plant. It has been tried over many years on a long list of conditions but at present there is insufficient evidence to prove effectiveness. In many instances the potential to kill the patient is as great a threat as the condition being treated. The search for more cancer treatments has yielded some potential value in Oleander for at least four cancers, including prostate and breast cancer, but there are yet to be trials on humans. For the present we exploit Oleander for insecticides and rat poison.

Most of the plants we grow for a touch of the exotic are of course kept indoors and few are seriously toxic. However, the constant search by the horticulture industry for something new to promote means that the range of plants on offer is greater than our general knowledge of them so caution is needed. Recently there has been a lot of media coverage over the deaths of cats after licking their fur clean of **Lily** (*Lilium*) pollen. Tomorrow there will be a new lead story.

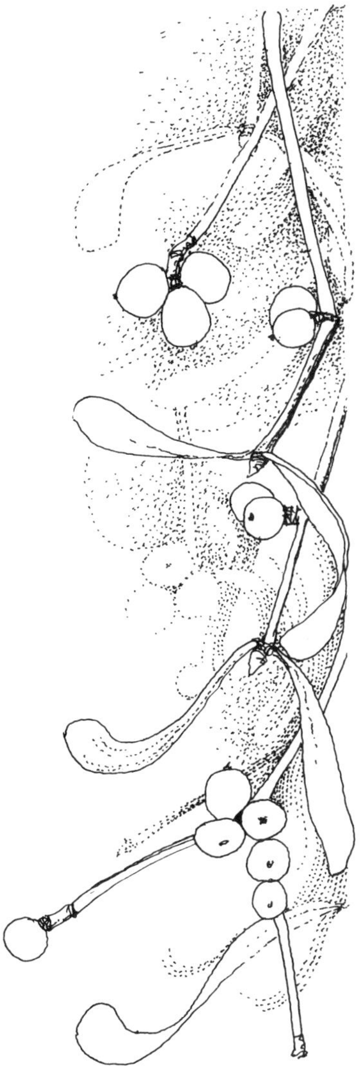

One house plant that surprised me was the **Swiss Cheese Plant** (*Monstera deliciosa* Liebm.), which I expected to yield a stack of toxicity reports, since a television programme showed South American natives smearing the juice on arrow heads for shooting down monkeys from the high canopy of the tropical rain forest. Such results did not turn up. Instead we read that biting into a leaf produces such intense pain in the mouth (from the needle-like crystals of calcium oxalate) that further consumption is abandoned. The same compound occurs again in the **Dumb Cane** or **Leopard Lily** (*Dieffenbachia spp.*) so once again it is the sap that causes trouble – severe local irritation and inflammation if you get in on your skin. It is certainly not something to try nibbling but pets do, so take this into account when choosing house plants. An even more popular one, with caustic sap, is the **Poinsettia** (*Euphorbia pulcherrima* Willd.ex Klotzsch.) but fortunately it is quite widely known for being hazardous. Actually it is not as toxic as its reputation (it contains diterpene esters). Nevertheless it is a Euphorbia and so the sap may cause dermatitis and should not be smeared in the eyes and mouth. Poinsettias are mass-produced for the Christmas market and so let us conclude with a few words on the other Christmas decorations.

**Mistletoe** (*Viscum album* L.) berries worry people at Christmas but usually a child would need to consume a lot of berries to present a case for serious concern. The stems and leaves are more toxic but being so tough and leathery are not palatable. Inside the berries there is an amazing collection of compounds but not all of these have been explored scientifically to the full. Many have a noticeable action in our bodies and have been used ritually and in medicines since prehistoric times. The active compounds include alkaloids, proteins and lectins, with the main poisons being called viscotoxin. Collectively they have diverse effects upon our bodies but some have a noticeable action upon our central nervous system, so Mistletoe berry usage has ranged from treating vertigo to anxiety and epilepsy. Obviously getting the dosage right is crucial when it comes to the brain and so although these medicines can temporarily numb the nervous system and thereby control epileptic spasms, too much of the stuff has the reverse effect. Today the Mistletoe berry compounds are used to calm a wide range of nervous complaints, from easing anxiety to calming hysteria and panic attacks. They thereby promote a good night's sleep and reduce nervous headaches. Collectively they can produce a good sense of well-being and that was obviously known to the Iron Age people since archaeologists have found the preserved remains of Mistletoe in the last meal eaten by the human sacrifices known as the 'Bog People'. Where the faces of these people have been

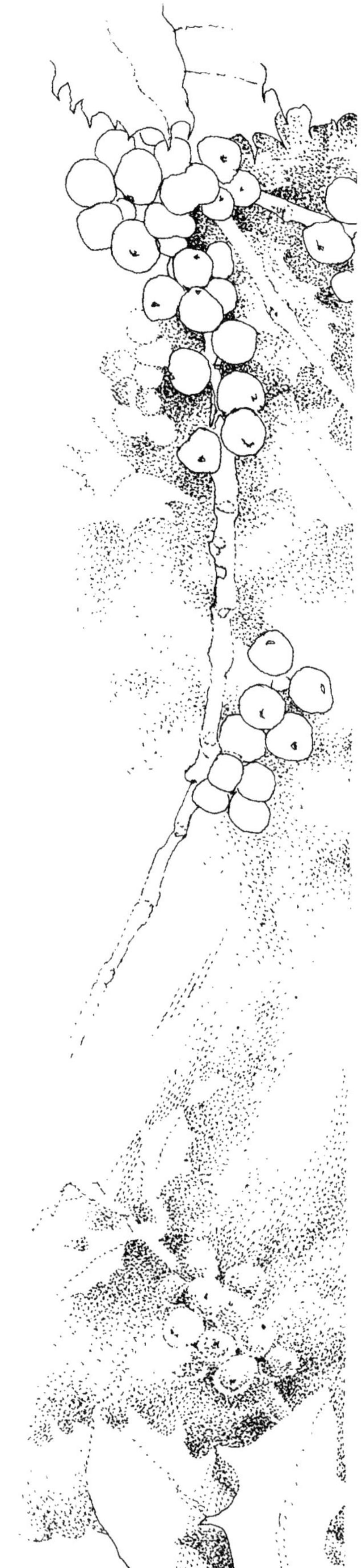

preserved they show a wonderful calm countenance. The Mistletoe would have lowered their blood pressure and heart rate too and this is still an important application over 2,000 years later. Today we are also exploring the berries for possible cancer treatments. To this end, attention is concentrating upon the lectins and whether they can be employed to combine with cancerous cells and prevent them taking up protein, but the world of lectins is diverse and complicated as indeed is the story of Mistletoe berries as known to science so far. Only a few brief highlights are given here. The important thing is to remember that the berries, wonderful as they are, contain poisons. The viscotoxins are closely related to polypeptides and those are what make the venom of some spiders so virulent.

**Holly** berries are the other Christmas concern and indeed they too are poisonous. They contain the cyanogenic glycoside ilicin but a lot of berries would need to be consumed before a dangerous amount could be absorbed into the body and this is mitigated against by the berries being emetic, so a child is likely to vomit out the berries. Where symptoms of poisoning have occurred toxicologists have wondered whether this is due to excessive brain stimulation from the content of caffeine and theobromine.

## Last Words

Further information on Holly can be found back at the beginning of this celebration of the poisonous plants in our everyday lives, for we have now travelled through the whole growing year. It has been a journey of great discoveries and many surprises. Also there have been dilemmas – should the book stress the dangers of using **Oleander** twigs as meat skewers for the garden barbeque? There was a lot on the Internet about families who have done this in the United States, with dire results, but this book is for Britain. We minimised that warning and now just two days ago the News reported a family in England who had done the same. The world of poisonous plants is changing all the time. We know from so many reports on the Internet that there is much research being conducted into these plants as we seek new foods and new medicines. The latter concentrates very much upon cancer treatments but in due course another concern will no doubt come to the fore and open up another window into the plant kingdom. Today there are thousands of people suffering from tuberculosis in Britain for whom the existing antibiotics are of little value, yet our herbals are full of plants used against TB in the past. Could there possibly be a treatment awaiting rediscovery in that list? Finding new medicines is such a slow (and expensive) business and little of the work nowadays starts with plants. Scientists work with models of molecules instead, engineering them to fit together in ways that have desired effects. Even so, plants can give clues for starting points. Susan Bond Horwitz marvelled at the structure of the anti-cancer molecules from Yew trees saying they were so bizarre that no scientists would have thought of engineering them in a laboratory. Work continues and so no final chapter to this book could ever be written.

I cannot resist ending with an illustration
of a graveyard monument at
Merstham in Surrey,
and the words
'Mind how you go.'

## SOURCES AND GUIDANCE

This book has been compiled from our own database, compiled over many years. Originally the best text we had for reference was a small paperback issued by the Ministry of Agriculture. Happily that was replaced by the Ministry with the much larger *Poisonous Plants in Britain and their Effects upon Animals and Man* by Marion Cooper and Anthony Johnson (1984; HMSO) which has proved invaluable ever since, especially as there is a bibliography of scientific papers for each plant. That book has now been updated as *Poisonous Plants and Fungi in Britain. Animal and Human Poisoning.* (1998); Second Edition; The Stationery Office Books.

Internet websites have been used to verify doubts and questions and to seek the latest research results. Several hundred have been used and so they are not listed here to save space for text. In any case, many are transitory and could be superseded by the latest research. Any readers seeking the latest information should be careful to search using the Latin name of the plant, since other names apply to differing plants around the world. Many plant names have synonyms and to seek that in current use we have referred to *The New Royal Horticultural Society Dictionary of Gardening;* ed. Anthony Huxley (1992, MacMillan); *New Flora of the British Isles;* Clive Stace (1991; CUP) and *Alien Plants of the British Isles* by E. Clement and M. Foster (1994; BSBI). For checking some botanical details, habitat and world distribution I used my old *Flora of the British Isles* by A. R. Clapham, Tutin and Warburg (1962; CUP).

Having found the Internet websites, readers are advised to reduce them to those published by the most responsible authorities (otherwise you will encounter masses of material that can sometimes be biased, misleading and lacking accuracy). If you are in Britain, search for reports that apply to Britain, remembering that the toxicity of some species varies from country to country. With this in mind, beware of culinary recipes and home remedies. For medicines always seek professional advice and remember to enquire about possible side-effects and contrary actions to any other medicines being taken. This book has reviewed the plants exploited in 'standard' medicine, not from the viewpoint of herbalism and homeopathy, etc.

### Garden

Britain's only garden devoted to poisonous plants is at Alnwick Castle, Northumberland.

### Illustrations

These have been culled from sketchbooks going back to the early 1970s. To save debate, the landscapes of specific places are as follows:

pp. 8&9 Flower market, East London
p.48 Derbyshire top; central Wales,
N. W. Sussex bottom
p.58 Construction of M25; Lyne Bridge,
near Junction 11
pp.62-3 Approach to Newport Docks, Gwent
p.73 Chepstow Castle, Gwent
p.74 Leatherhead Bridge, Surrey
p.83 View from window, Guildford, Surrey
p.84 Alfold, Surrey
p.85 Thorpe, Surrey
p.87 George Eliot's 'Brookbank', Haslemere,
Surrey
p.102 View from window, Crich, Derbyshire
p.106 two views, Ware, Hertfordshire

## INDEX